Comments on other *Amazing* ᵕ

"*Tightly written volumes filled with lots of wit and humour about famous and infamous Canadians.*"
Eric Shackleton, *The Globe and Mail*

"*The heightened sense of drama and intrigue, combined with a good dose of human interest is what sets* Amazing Stories *apart.*"
Pamela Klaffke, *Calgary Herald*

"*This is popular history as it should be... For this price, buy two and give one to a friend.*"
Terry Cook, a reader from Ottawa, on **Rebel Women**

"*Glasner creates the moment of the explosion itself in graphic detail...she builds detail upon gruesome detail to create a convincingly authentic picture.*"
Peggy McKinnon, *The Sunday Herald,* on **The Halifax Explosion**

"*It was wonderful...I found I could not put it down. I was sorry when it was completed.*"
Dorothy F. from Manitoba on **Marie-Anne Lagimodière**

"*Stories are rich in description, and bristle with a clever, stylish realness.*"
Mark Weber, *Central Alberta Advisor,* on **Ghost Town Stories II**

"*A compelling read. Bertin...has selected only the most intriguing tales, which she narrates with a wealth of detail.*"
Joyce Glasner, *New Brunswick Reader,* on **Strange Events**

"*The resulting book is one readers will want to share with all the women in their lives.*"
Lynn Martel, *Rocky Mountain Outlook,* on **Women Explorers**

GREY OWL

AMAZING STORIES

GREY OWL

The Curious Life of Archie Belaney

BIOGRAPHY

by Irene Ternier Gordon

PUBLISHED BY ALTITUDE PUBLISHING CANADA LTD.
1500 Railway Avenue, Canmore, Alberta T1W 1P6
www.altitudepublishing.com
1-800-957-6888

Extreme care has been taken to ensure that all information presented in
this book is accurate and up to date. Neither the author nor the
publisher can be held responsible for any errors.

Publisher	Stephen Hutchings
Associate Publisher	Kara Turner
Series Editor	Jill Foran
Editor	Anita Jenkins
Digital photo colouring & map	Scott Manktelow

We acknowledge the financial support of the Government
of Canada through the Book Publishing Industry Development
Program (BPIDP) for our publishing activities.

Altitude GreenTree Program
Altitude Publishing will plant twice as many trees as were used
in the manufacturing of this product.

We acknowledge the support of the Canada Council for the Arts which
in 2003 invested $21.7 million in writing and publishing throughout Canada.

Canada Council   Conseil des Arts
for the Arts   du Canada

National Library of Canada Cataloguing in Publication Data

Gordon, Irene
Grey Owl / Irene Gordon.

(Amazing stories)
Includes bibliographical references.
ISBN 1-55153-785-0

1. Grey Owl, 1888-1938. 2. Conservationists--Canada--Biography.
3. Authors, Canadian (English)--20th century--Biography. I. Title. II.
Series: Amazing stories (Canmore, Alta.)

FC541.G75G67 2004   639.9'092   C2004-902321-7

An application for the trademark for Amazing Stories™
has been made and the registered trademark is pending.

Printed and bound in Canada by Friesens
2 4 6 8 9 7 5 3 1

To everyone who shares my love for the rivers and lakes of the Canadian wilderness — especially to my husband Don and the relatives and friends with whom we have shared so many sailing and canoeing trips over the years.

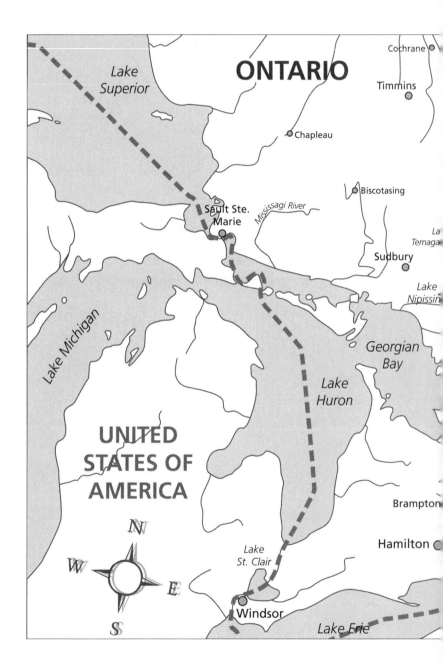

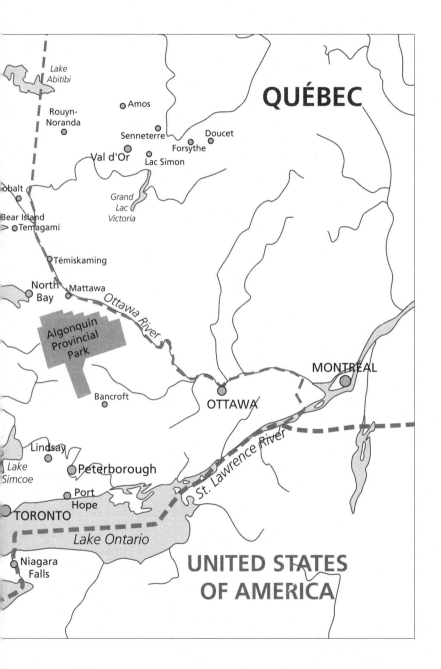

Contents

Prologue

Suddenly Archie heard an ominous sound. It was a sound to strike terror in anyone walking across a frozen lake — cracking ice! Before he could take evasive action, Archie found himself sinking into the icy water.

Thankfully, Archie managed to grab hold of a large stick protruding from the ice and pull himself onto a solid surface within seconds. But the damage was already done. Archie was wet half-way to his knees. Unless he dried his feet they would begin to freeze almost immediately, and he couldn't make a fire where he was. The area was too exposed and smoke would attract the rangers. Surely, though, in a place as hilly and well-treed as Algonquin Park, he could quickly reach a suitable place to make a fire.

He set off at a brisk pace, but soon realized that the closest trees were much farther away than they appeared. He was shivering violently and it was becoming an effort to move one snowshoe in front of the other as numbness crept up his legs. He knew he had no choice but to risk a fire in the open.

Archie cursed himself for the bravado that had landed him in this situation. After nearly three years in the Canadian wilderness, he had felt so confident that he had bet another trapper he could cross Algonquin Provincial Park in the dead of winter without the park rangers catching him. Since trapping was prohibited in the park, he would face a heavy fine if he were caught carrying traps and a gun.

He stopped, but it was already too late. When he attempted to gather kindling for a fire, his hands would not obey him. He collapsed and lay helpless in the gathering dusk. Was this to be the end of his Canadian adventure? He wondered if anyone would find him before spring.

Chapter 1
Arrival in Temagami

n August 1906 the train stopped at the Temagami station in northern Ontario. A slender young man named Archie Belaney stepped onto the platform. He was handsome, dark-haired, and over six feet tall, and he moved with the grace of a cat. For a few seconds he looked over the small crowd that had come to meet the train. Then he headed straight for the most grizzled and colourful-looking person on the platform, a guide named Bill Guppy who was known as "The King of the Woodsmen."

Archie, who was just 18 years old, told Bill that he wanted to become a guide — to learn to follow a trail, camp and cook in the woods, and skilfully steer a canoe through the rapids. It took only a few moments of Archie's considerable charm to captivate Bill, and they soon struck an agreement. Archie would move in with the Guppy family and work for Bill in return for room and board over the winter. Bill would teach Archie the survival skills and native lore he craved, so he could begin his longed-for life in the northern bush.

Such was Archie Belaney's introduction to the Temiskaming area, which is near the Quebec border. He had arrived in Canada from Sussex, England, only four months earlier.

Archie was raised by his widowed grandmother and two maiden aunts, Ada and Carrie, in the seaside town of Hastings. Archie's father, George, had been the spoiled darling of his mother and had grown up to be an alcoholic ne'er-do-well. George wasted so much of his family's fortune that Ada and Carrie convinced their mother to banish him before he left the family destitute. George was forced to sign a document that allowed him a small income on the condition that he never set foot in England again. George's American-born wife, Kitty, was promised an income to bring up their two sons, Archie and Hugh, provided she had no further contact with George.

When Archie was four years old, the Belaneys learned that Kitty had sent money to George once or twice, and they responded by stopping Kitty's income and taking Archie away from her. All anyone would ever tell Archie about his father was that he was somewhere in America. He rarely saw

A portrait of Archie aged 13 in Hastings, England

his mother and younger brother, who lived in London, and he was not close to them.

As a child, Archie had a passionate interest in two subjects — wild animals and North American native people —

and avidly read everything he could find about them. He spent long hours wandering through the rugged glens and woods around Hastings and observing the wildlife. He had an unusual affinity with wild animals, which seemed to enjoy being handled by him. He was allowed to keep a menagerie of animals in the attic of the family home, where he took great pains to create a natural environment for them. He was particularly fond of snakes. One of his snakes, a poisonous adder, bit him and he had to be rushed to hospital for treatment. Even after that, Archie was still allowed to keep poisonous snakes as long as he defanged them.

Archie's school yearbook described him as an 11-year-old who might produce a snake or field mouse from his pocket at any moment. "What with his camping out, his tracking all and sundry, and wild hooting," the yearbook said of Archie, "he was more like a Red Indian than a respectable Grammar School Boy." The term "wild hooting" was a bit of an exaggeration. Archie had already begun using a soft owl's call as a signal and would continue to do so throughout his life.

A highlight of Archie's adolescent life was attending Buffalo Bill's Wild West Show, which came to Hastings in 1903. He also began learning to shoot and throw knives. A former school mate remembered Archie telling the other boys that his parents lived in the American West and that he was going to join them when he left school.

His aunts reluctantly agreed that he could go to Canada when he left school if he worked for a year to save his fare. This was on the understanding that he would learn farming and work as a farmer until he turned 21. Then he could do what he wanted.

Aunt Ada found Archie a position as a clerk with a local firm of timber merchants, but he hated the job. He was fired after he let a small bag of gunpowder down the chimney in his employer's office. The resulting explosion almost demolished the office.

On his arrival in Canada, Archie got a job selling men's clothing at a large Toronto department store (likely Eaton's). After working there long enough to earn his train fare north, he headed for Cobalt, Ontario, where silver had been discovered in 1903. He had heard that there might be work in the area. It is not clear why he ended up at Temiskaming — perhaps because he was not interested in mining or he did not have the fare to travel farther.

Although Archie certainly spent his first Canadian winter with the Guppy family, a cryptic entry in one of his later notebooks indicates that he may actually have had a slightly different introduction to northern Ontario. The entry reads, "Early troubles at Cobalt and Temagami and being robbed at night...Sickness and broke. Befriended by Indians."

Years later, Archie told his wife Pony that he did not have enough money for a ticket all the way to Cobalt and had to get off the train about 80 kilometres from his destination without food or proper gear. He then walked for three days before falling sick and being rescued by one of the Bear

Island Ojibwa. Even during Archie's earliest days in Canada, his life was characterized by mystery and secrets.

Over the winter, the Guppy family became very fond of Archie. He was so articulate and well-spoken that they called him "Professor." They were delighted to discover that he was an excellent pianist. As Bill put it, he was "a wizard on the keys, rattling out tune after tune, and picking up the songs we sang."

Bill's two brothers taught Archie how to throw tomahawks and hunting knives at targets with pinpoint accuracy. Bill encouraged this pastime because he knew that this skill would set his boys apart from the other hunting guides, who were all vying for the tourist dollar. By the next summer, Archie was so skilful with axe and knife that tourists would pin money to a tree and challenge him. "You cut it in half, and it's yours."

The Guppy brothers and their two hired men (Archie and an Ojibwa man named Michel Mathias) made a number of trips during the winter by dog team to carry supplies to Lake Temagami, where Bill planned to build a small tourist camp the following summer. The men also did a lot of hard physical labour in preparing the site for construction. When it was too cold to handle an axe, Michel took Archie out on snowshoes to explore the surrounding area. Archie also began learning to interpret animal tracks. Although in many ways he was the proverbial "green Englishman," Archie already had an extensive knowledge of animals and a complete lack of fear. He would approach them as closely as possible and observe them for hours.

Bill gave Archie lessons in trapping. Archie was a born hunter, but he did have one weakness as hunter and trapper — he felt sorry for the animals.

Bill described how Archie reacted the first time he killed a beaver. The two men were crossing a lake when they saw a beaver on the ice. Bill explained that beavers stayed in their houses under the ice all winter, so this one must have accidentally come out and then got lost. Archie killed the beaver with a blow of his axe and triumphantly shouted, "Got you!" But when he picked up the beaver, his air of triumph disappeared almost immediately. He said, "It seems such a pity to kill them — but, oh well, we've got to live."

On another occasion Archie was to write to a friend, "I killed that lynx today and somehow I wished I hadn't. His skin is only worth $10...and the way he looked at me I can't get that out of my mind."

More experienced trappers were later to criticize Archie's trapping ability. They said that many of his furs were badly skinned and dried, and that he couldn't find half his traps after he set them because he failed to blaze his territory properly. He was also accused of having set a number of bear traps one spring and then not having gone back to pick them up. Whether these stories were true is impossible to say.

As soon as the lakes were clear of ice in early May, Archie and the Guppys left by canoe for Lake Temagami where they would spend the summer. Archie went through a baptism by fire on this journey, which was his first long canoe trip. They paddled some 50 kilometres to the first portage, called the Devil's Portage, which rose almost 500 metres above the river. Carrying a heavy pack or canoe was especially difficult early in the season while the steep path was still slippery from melting snow and water. This was the first of many trips Archie would make through the chain of lakes linking Lakes Temiskaming and Temagami. Within a few years he had gained a reputation as an expert canoeist.

Lake Temagami is one of the largest lakes in northeastern Ontario with more than 1200 islands and a shoreline of 1000 kilometres. Near the centre of the lake is Bear Island, site of a Hudson's Bay trading post and home to a band of Ojibwa. During that first summer, Archie worked as a chore boy at the Temagami Inn across from Bear Island since he didn't yet have enough experience to be a guide.

That fall, Archie decided not to return to Temiskaming with the Guppys. He had made friends with some of the Bear Island people, and he asked the Hudson's Bay factor for a grubstake so he could go trapping with them. The factor turned him down because he lacked trapping experience, but Bill Guppy arranged for him to be appointed the mail carrier between Temiskaming and Temagami for several winters.

Soon after his arrival at Temagami, Archie met Angele Eguana, a young woman from one of the most prominent Bear Island families. They both had summer jobs at the Temagami Inn and likely met there.

Archie got to know Angele's family very well as a result

of an incident that occurred while he was delivering mail. When a snarling husky rushed towards him on the trail, Archie stretched out his hands to the dog, and it suddenly changed into a fawning pet. A few minutes later, two women came along — one was elderly and the other was young and beautiful. The women spoke little English, but they made Archie understand that the dog had been pulling a baby on a sleigh when somehow he had slipped out of his harness and run off.

Archie accompanied the women to Temagami, along with the baby who had slept peacefully through all the excitement. The young woman was Angele, and the older one was her grandmother, Old Lady Cat. They invited Archie to visit them at the home of Angele's aunt, who could speak English. Archie and Angele got to know each other over the winter with the help of the aunt's translation services. Archie also began learning to speak Ojibwa, and he listened with interest to Old Lady Cat's tales about the old days.

Angele's uncle John Eguana began to call Archie Ko-hom-see or Little Owl, "the young owl who sits taking everything in." Archie would sit for hours listening to stories and making notes in a small book he always carried with him. John joked that Archie was so fair you could see him coming for miles, "just like when you make a blaze on a tree."

Archie met another interesting character on Bear Island — a man known as Both-Ends-of-the-Day or Temagami Ned. He later wrote about Ned in *The Men of the Last Frontier*.

Ned's name came from his unusually developed faculty for seeing in the dark. Day and night were all one to him.

Instead of a pocket watch, Ned carried an alarm clock inside his shirt. He once fell asleep at a dance, and a mischievous youngster set the alarm. Ned created the diversion of the evening when the sudden racket woke him up. In reality, though, the child's first touch had awakened him. He went along with the joke, pretending to sleep until the alarm went off.

In the summer of 1908 Archie applied to the Temagami justice of the peace for a licence to marry Angele Eguana but then left before the marriage took place. The desk clerk at the Temagami Lodge told of seeing Archie paddling away in a canoe with half a dozen Ojibwa canoes in pursuit. Archie later told someone that Angele's family came after him with tomahawks.

Most likely, Archie was having second thoughts about marriage and was trying to enjoy its privileges without taking on any of its responsibilities. He disappeared from northern Ontario and was not seen again until late in the winter of 1909. He apparently returned to England for three months during that time.

In March 1909 Archie made a bet that he could cross Algonquin Park without the park rangers catching him. An important part of the rangers' work was to prevent poaching in the park, so when Park Superintendent George Bartlett learned about the bet he sent two rangers after Archie.

At first everything went well for Archie. He followed the setting sun as closely as possible, veering off only when an obstacle prevented him from taking the direct route. Then, coming down a hill, he saw two depressions divided by a rough track. He assumed they indicated a lake divided by a narrow strip of land, so he followed the shortcut across rather than go around the shoreline.

Suddenly Archie heard the ominous sound of cracking ice and found himself knee-deep in icy water. He grabbed hold of a large stick protruding from the ice and managed to pull himself onto a solid surface within seconds. But the damage was already done. He had been walking across the roofs of beaver lodges and not on dry land. Archie realized that unless he dried his feet they would begin to freeze almost immediately. He knew he had no choice but to start a fire in the open and risk discovery by the rangers.

Ranger Mark Robinson, one of the two men Bartlett sent to track Archie, recorded these events in his diary. The rangers set off on March 15 and travelled for three days without seeing any trace of their quarry. Then they met two other rangers, who had come across the severely frostbitten Archie just in time to save his life. The four men took him to park headquarters, and Bartlett ordered Robinson to conduct Archie out of the park as soon as he was fit to travel. Robinson wrote, "Mr. Belaney used up in the feet with frost. Decided to keep him until Monday." Archie kept the rangers well entertained with his stories, and Bartlett did not fine him since he hadn't set any traps.

While Robinson's diary indicated that Archie was well enough to travel after four days, other reports stated that he was laid up for three weeks and that Superintendent Bartlett got two beef galls from the local butcher to wrap around his swollen feet to reduce the pain.

Archie soon made up with Angele, and they were married the following year, in August 1910. The ceremony was performed by a visiting American clergyman. Archie worked as a guide at Camp Keewaydin on Lake Temagami during the summers of 1910 and 1911. Here he taught 11 and 12-year-old American prep school boys about fishing, canoeing, and what was then called "Indian lore." Working at Camp Keewaydin would have appealed to Archie on two counts. Keewaydin was the name of the northwest wind in one of his favourite poems, "The Song of Hiawatha" by Henry Wadsworth Longfellow. Also, the camp director based his program on Ernest Thompson Seton's books on native lore, which Archie had read in his boyhood. Camp Keewaydin, founded in Maine in 1893 and moved to Lake Temagami in 1902, is still in operation. It claims to be the oldest continuously operating summer camp in North America.

Until the 1890s the Bear Island Ojibwa had lived in the traditional way and had little contact with the outside world, except for yearly visits from a missionary priest and an Indian agent. But now the Ontario government was imposing all sorts of rules on the native people and leasing islands in the lake to build tourist camps and private cottages. Archie knew tourism would create jobs for the local people, but still he despised these changes. He believed the Ojibwa would become mere servants in their own land.

Archie agreed with Bear Island chief Aleck Paul, who said in 1913, "If an Indian went to the old country and sold hunting licenses to the old country people for them to hunt on their own land, the white people would not stand for that. The Government sells our big game...our fish and our islands and gets the money but we don't get any share."

Angele and Archie's daughter, Agnes, was born in April 1911, but Archie was unable to cope with either marriage or fatherhood. That fall he left his family and went north to Lake Abitibi with three other trappers. There is some evidence that he may have spent only a few months trapping and the rest of the winter in Toronto and Montreal. At any rate, he returned penniless to Angele in the spring and told her he had walked from Toronto. He didn't explain what had happened over the winter or why he had no money after a winter of supposed trapping.

Archie's account of his experiences at Lake Abitibi was later published as an article in the newsletter of his old school. This article about the life of woodsmen and trappers reflected the superior attitude people of European descent have often displayed towards aboriginal people. Since none of Archie's behaviour or other writings during his life expressed such views, he was likely trying to impress those he had left at home or to make the story more humorous.

For example, the following passage from the article seems to contradict Archie's obvious admiration for the Ojibwa, his enthusiasm for learning to speak their language, and his awareness that he and his friends had set their traps in someone else's trapping territory.

...three other fellows persuaded me that the happy hunting grounds...[were] located in the country north of the Abitibi Lake...We were all fixed up and our traps out in the best hunting country we could find, when Mr. Indian appears on the starboard bow, and remarks that...our appearance on the scene is both obnoxious and unnecessary. Fortunately, I can murder the beautiful flowing gutturals and meat-axe noises made by the red brother, and was able to converse with our new-found friend...

The article ended on a more serious note, but again it put forward different views than those Archie would express in most of his later writing: "It looks very picturesque and romantic to wear moccasins, run rapids, and shoot deer and moose, but it is not near as interesting as it seems, to be eaten up day and night by black ants, flies and mosquitoes, to get soaked up with rain and burnt up with heat. To draw your own toboggan on snow-shoes, and to sleep out in 60 or 70 degrees below zero."

Archie remained with Angele and baby Agnes for three

or four more weeks in the summer of 1912 but then left again. He told Angele that he would return in the fall, but she didn't see him again for six years. Occasionally he would send her small sums of money, but she largely supported herself and Agnes by trapping.

Chapter 2
More or Less a Renegade

hen Archie left Angele he moved to Biscotasing, some 160 kilometres west of Temagami. The town, founded in 1885 by the Canadian Pacific Railway, was a fur trade and distribution centre for the Hudson's Bay Company and a base for government forest rangers. Until the outbreak of the First World War in 1914, Archie worked as a fire ranger in the nearby Mississauga Forest Reserve in the summer and trapped in the winter. He was fond of Biscotasing and of the couple of hundred people who lived there in small wooden houses scattered along the rocky hillside of a sheltered bay on Biscotasing Lake. Seemingly limitless forest stretched out in all directions from the lake.

When he was in town Archie roomed at Matilda Legace's boarding house. Her son recalled that initially Archie was polite and friendly to everyone, and people frequently invited him over for a meal or to spend the evening. Upon closer acquaintance, though, Archie was not quite so popular. He began using profanity and rough language, drank too much, and got into fights. Matilda Legace was a large woman who had a lot of experience in dealing with unruly boarders. When Archie misbehaved, she would say to him sternly, "That's enough, Archie, or I'll hit you over the head." Archie listened to her.

A young native woman named Marie Girard worked as a maid in Mrs. Legace's boarding house. Although she knew he was married, Marie fell hard for the handsome and sensitive Archie who played the piano so wonderfully. So when he invited Marie to spend the winter of 1913-14 with him on his trap line, she accepted.

Harry Woodsworth, the Hudson's Bay factor and local law officer, thought Archie spent too much time practicing shooting and knife throwing and that he later "became more or less of a renegade." Although Woodsworth tried to have Archie arrested on several occasions, Archie later wrote that, despite his strictness in upholding the law, Woodsworth had "a heart as big as a barrel" and that he would "...go the prisoner's bail, feed him, house him, take a drink with him and generally provide what was probably the most efficient...police service to be found anywhere in North America...."

By the time Archie arrived in Bisco he was a skilled canoeist who felt completely at home on the water. In *Tales of an Empty Cabin*, he lovingly described a typical canoe trip on the Mississagi River (which he usually spelled "Mississauga"). The day began early when the brigade chief woke his men by slapping smartly on their tents and shouting that it was after three and time to get up to see to their canoes. The men might grumble, but Archie's tent-mate Red Landreville joked about it, saying the canoes must be awfully wild if it was necessary to creep up on them under cover of darkness. The men prepared breakfast in pairs, with one tea pail and a frying pan for every two men. Some mornings, Billy Mitchell, who was justly proud of his cooking skills, offered to make what he called "community pancakes" for everyone.

Bannock (a type of biscuit made of flour, baking powder, lard, salt and water) was the staple of their diet. It could be cooked in a frying pan, baked in an oven, or wrapped around a stick and cooked over a campfire. Other provisions included salt pork, tea, sugar, dried white beans, and dried apples. This monotonous fare was augmented by freshly caught fish and whatever berries were in season. These old-time canoeists, Archie said, looked down on those who carried such luxuries as butter, jam, and canned goods. Jam had an uncomfortable way of coming open and mixing with the other supplies, canned goods were too heavy, and it was impossible to keep butter from turning to oil in hot weather.

Archie described the love-hate relationship between

the rangers and their chiefs. The rangers discreetly thumbed their noses at the chiefs but at the same time broke their backs "to fulfil and sometimes exceed" the chief's orders. They loved to boast about how many miles they could paddle in a day and how many pounds they could carry per trip on a portage. While admiringly introducing his fellow rangers, Archie also summed up his own philosophy. He wrote: "How I loved them for their sharp-barbed, gritty humour, their unparalleled skill in profanity, their easy-going generosity...White man, red-skin and half-breed, they belonged to that fraternity of freemen of the earth whose creed it is that all men are born equal, and that it is up to a man to stay that way. For in this society the manner of a man's speech, where he comes from, his religion, or even his name are matters of small moment and are nobody's business but his own."

Archie described the proper paddling technique:

...grip the canoe ribs with your knees, drive those paddles deep, throw your weight on to them, click them on those gunnels twenty-five strokes to the minute...bend those backs, and drive!

Steersman, keep your eyes on the far objective...and take your proper allowance for a side-wind, don't make leeway like a greenhorn! Thus, eyes fixed ahead, watchful of everything, breath coming deeply, evenly, backs swinging freely from the hips, paddles dipping and flashing, we drive her — fifty miles a day or bust.

Late one day, Archie recalled, the rangers had two minor accidents at portages. First, a man named Baldy fell and bloodied his nose when his tumpline broke. (The tumpline is a leather strap that passes over the forehead and is used to support a load carried on the back.) No one was sympathetic to the blood-covered Baldy, who complained bitterly about his defective tumpline. The other men had all previously told him that he was trying to carry too heavy a load and that his tumpline was getting old and worn out.

The second accident occurred when a man named Matogense was knocked off a log bridge into a bog by another man carrying a canoe. Here again, no one was sympathetic. The men recalled the story about how Matogense's daughter was supposedly fed live fish to help her learn to swim. One wag suggested giving Matogense a frog to eat so he could get around better in the mud.

To everyone's relief, after Matogense's accident the chief decided it was time to make camp for the night. It was getting close to dark and the men were all tired.

Archie described the scene: "Camp is quickly made within an encircling grove of giant red-pines, whose crenellated columns, all ruddy in the firelight, stand about the place like huge pillars that support a roof so high above us as to be invisible…giving us the feeling that we are encamped in some old, deserted temple."

Tents were pitched, supper prepared and eaten, bannock made for the next day, and everything stowed, ready for the morning. Then the men had an hour of quiet relaxation before bed. There were no sounds save the crackle of the campfire and the murmur of voices as the men sat around the camp fire. At such times the talk always turned to reminiscences of earlier days.

Many tales were told about Dan O'Connor, pioneer Temagami resort owner, who would do almost anything to boost tourism. On one occasion a railway magnate looking for a place with good duck hunting was visiting Temagami. While Temagami did have good duck hunting in the fall, the man visited in mid-summer when there were no ducks around. Dan ordered some domestic ducks from the city and arranged for a local man to shoot them and carry them past the hotel where Dan and the railway magnate were staying. The railway man "was treated, in a wilderness removed a hundred and fifty miles from any farm, to the astounding spectacle of a round dozen of common barnyard ducks, tastefully arranged upon a pole."

The most exciting part of any canoe trip was running the rapids. At the head of the rapids, the rangers unloaded half the goods from each canoe, leaving only gear that the water would not damage. Then they paddled into the centre of the river, set the canoes at the proper angle and took off. Archie described it as follows:

The canoes seem to leap suddenly ahead, and one after another, with a wild, howling hurrah, we are into the thick of it. Huge combers [waves], any one of which would swamp a canoe, stand...terrifically beside us, close enough to touch. The backlash from one of these smashes against the bows and we are slashed in the face by what seems to be a ton of water...there is a thunderous roar which envelopes us like a tunnel, a last flying leap and we are in the still pool below...thrilled to the bone.

Although Archie could be touchy and bad-tempered, he could also laugh at himself on occasion. He told how he and another man had once upset their canoe in front of a large audience of fellow rangers while going down some rapids. Archie hung onto the stern of the canoe and travelled to the end of the rapids "like the tail of a comet." Meanwhile the bowsman, who almost drowned when his foot become wedged under the canoe, managed to free himself. He climbed onto the canoe, which promptly sank with Archie still holding onto it.

Because Archie couldn't swim, he clung desperately to the canoe, hoping it would float upward again. When his head finally broke water, another canoe was racing towards him, the paddler shouting encouragement. Suddenly, to Archie's horror, the paddler stopped, began to laugh and shouted, "Why don't you stand up?"

He did so and discovered that the water didn't even reach his waist.

One of Archie's fellow river men/rangers later said that

most people thought Archie was a great showman who possibly had "a streak of Indian in him." The ranger said that in addition to showing off with "all kinds of Indian stunts" such as throwing knives, Archie "…was in his glory when reciting original poetry, and after giving one of those pieces he would say: 'That's by Bill Shakespeare, Tennyson, Browning, etc.,' and laugh. He seemed a remarkably likeable man who, even in those days, wanted to hide his past."

If people asked Archie why he wore his hair long, he would say he let it grow out of pride in his connection with the Apache. Already in those years before the First World War, Archie was telling people he had been born in Mexico. He said his parents were a Scotsman named George MacNeil and an Apache woman named Katherine Cochise. He claimed his father had been an Indian scout in the American southwest and that his parents later joined Buffalo Bill's Wild West Show. He accounted for his English accent by saying that his father's English sisters had arranged for his education while his parents were touring in England with Buffalo Bill in 1903. He even claimed that some of his father's Scottish cousins had a letter from Buffalo Bill that spoke very highly of "my Dad." People who had met Archie soon after he arrived in Canada, when he still had a strong English accent, knew those stories could not be true. But others believed them.

Because Archie was working in a very remote area during the summer of 1914, he didn't learn until six weeks later that the First World War had broken out in early August.

When he finally arrived back in Bisco he immediately got drunk and badly damaged the lumber company boarding house. He also celebrated his return by shooting off his rifle and throwing knives at human targets. Woodsworth, as Bisco's law officer, called for police from a neighbouring town to arrest Archie.

Archie had to leave town to avoid arrest, and he asked Marie Girard to join him again. They hid out in the woods for several months before Archie abandoned her and disappeared from the area entirely.

Chapter 3
The Injured Foot

othing more was heard from Archie until he enlisted in the army at Digby, Nova Scotia, on May 16, 1915. Shortly afterwards he wrote to a friend in Bisco saying that he was waiting to go overseas. He sent some money from his army pay to be given to Marie Girard. He also wrote to the manager of the Bear Island Hudson's Bay Post, asking him to tell Angele he was going overseas, but he did not send her any money and on his enlistment papers he indicated that he was single. As a result Angele did not receive the military pay she was entitled to as the wife of an enlisted man.

Marie Girard gave birth to a son, Johnny, in the fall of 1915 and died of tuberculosis shortly afterwards. Many people in Bisco thought that Archie had treated Marie and Johnny very badly. Archie made no effort to see Johnny, who was raised by a local family, or to provide financial support while he was growing up.

Almost 20 years later Archie told a friend that he had actually first enlisted in Montreal in late 1914 or early in the winter of 1915, but had deserted before enlisting again in Digby. No record of his enlistment in Montreal has been found under either Belaney or McNeil. But when he applied for Canadian citizenship in 1934, Archie stated again that he had joined the Canadian Army in November 1914.

In Digby, Archie claimed to have had previous military experience in Mexico and was consequently made a lance-corporal. A month later he left for England. His career as a lance-corporal soon ended, though. He went AWOL — apparently to visit his aunts — and was demoted to private.

Despite his demotion, Archie impressed at least one of his officers in England. Lieutenant Banks, scouting instructor for the Canadian 23rd Reserve Battalion, said, "His maps and reports were so remarkable that I would show them to the colonel…and they would be handed around to the officers."

Archie now added some new details to his life story. He told people he had been forced to leave Mexico in a hurry after shooting a man who had murdered a member of his family — in some stories it was his brother and in others his Texas Ranger father.

In late August 1915 Archie was transferred to the 13th

The Injured Foot

Montreal (Black Watch) Battalion and sent to the trenches of Flanders. He was not impressed when he learned that he would have to wear a kilt. He had asked Lieutenant Banks to look after his pair of six-shooters until he shipped out. When Banks went to Archie's tent to return his guns, he found Archie very upset. "Here was Belaney, with tears in his eyes, holding up a pair of kilts and telling me that an Indian could not wear women's skirts."

In Flanders, Archie's platoon commander decided to make him a sniper-observer. The commander recalled, "He had infinite patience and the gift of absolute immobility for long periods. His reports as an observer were short, to the point, and intelligent. Unlike many snipers, he did not make exaggerated claims of 'kills.' Belaney was a dependable, if not an outstanding soldier…"

Archie found military life difficult, but he showed reckless courage. There is a story about how he made his way to a shelled farmhouse standing in the no-man's land between the lines and returned with a sack of vegetables and a bottle of wine. No one spotted him during the hour and a half he was gone.

In January 1916 Archie received a bullet wound in the wrist. He went back into action almost immediately but in April suffered a foot wound. This time, gangrene set in. He spent more than a year in various English hospitals (including four months at the Canadian Military Hospital in Hastings) and finally had one toe amputated. His lungs had also been damaged by mustard gas.

It is hard to imagine how Archie must have felt when he found himself in hospital in his home town of Hastings, a place that had left him with so few happy childhood memories.

Archie's grandmother, who led the retired life of an upper middle-class Victorian widow, had left most of Archie's upbringing to her younger daughter Ada. He later told his wife Pony that he had loved his grandmother and Carrie but hated the domineering Ada. Archie said Ada was a perfectionist and disciplinarian who "lacked a human heart" and "was obsessed with turning me into some kind of genius." Archie admitted grudgingly, "I suppose in her way she loved me, or she wouldn't have given so much of herself towards my upbringing."

Still, he claimed that Ada made his childhood such a hell that he even thought of committing suicide several times. He said he once tried to kill her by hitting her with a heavy bust of Bach that stood between two huge potted plants in an alcove. His plot backfired when the bust hit him on the head instead and knocked him out.

He blamed Ada for his bad behaviour as an adult, and undoubtedly his lack of a male role model while growing up was a factor in his inability to successfully handle either marriage or fatherhood. Archie described the situation this way:

She'd have liked...to break my spirit. Luckily I put up a fight, and she succeeded only in making a devil out of me...

The Injured Foot

When I first came to live in the bush...I used to get a kick out of doing what I knew would have horrified her. But sometimes I got carried away and did things that even I felt were wrong, and that gave me a lot more satisfaction....

It is not surprising that Archie told people that he had been raised in Mexico because one of his few happy childhood memories was receiving a gift of a miniature Mexican ranch from his father when he was about five years old. He was able to vividly describe it in later years. "I thought it was the most wonderful thing in the world, and it was. It had the little adobe houses, stables, and carved wooden horses — they had Navajo blankets instead of saddles on their backs — and little Mexican figures. Two of these figures I picked out as being my father and me, and I used to spend hour upon hour...imagining that he and I were working together on our ranch."

Several years after Archie arrived in Canada, his mother wrote to tell him that his father had died in the United States. Kitty believed he had been killed in a drunken brawl, but it is unlikely she told Archie that.

While in hospital Archie reconnected with Ivy Holmes, with whom he had shared a brief teenage romance. Ivy was a beautiful woman who had become a professional dancer and had toured throughout Europe for six years after Archie went to Canada. Ivy later wrote, "He had all the glamour of a wounded soldier. Lines of pain had given character to his dark handsome face…We fell violently in love."

After Archie got out of hospital, he married Ivy — despite the fact that he was still legally married to Angele. The realization that it would be impossible to bring Ivy back to northern Ontario created tremendous conflict for Archie, and Ivy quickly began to find him secretive and almost sinister.

In September 1917 Archie sailed back to Canada where he was given a medical discharge from the army and a 20 per cent disability pension. He received regular therapy as an outpatient in Toronto over the winter, but his foot continued to give him trouble. A May 1918 medical report stated: "Right foot same as before. Cannot walk 1 mile on pavements without pain. Can walk four or five miles on snowshoes. Can walk a couple of miles in bush, but cannot do any packing."

His foot improved slowly, but both his foot and his lungs continued to give Archie trouble for the remainder of his life. When Archie went trapping during the winter of 1919–20, he had to spend 30 minutes or more every morning dressing his foot.

The war also took a psychological toll. Archie had been in some of the worst trench warfare and had killed enemy soldiers as a sniper. Years later he told a friend that one night he had hung his coat on a tree branch, only to discover in the daylight that he had used the arm of a dead man for a coat rack. Archie's younger brother Hugh was driven mad by his war experiences and spent the remainder of his life in an institution.

Shortly after Archie returned home to Canada, he went to visit Angele and their daughter Agnes. Angele later described the visit. "I sleep with him that night. I think four days he stay...Happy. I just think I got married that day. Feel that way anyway. I love that man and I love him still." She did not see him again for eight years.

Ivy was supposed to join Archie in Canada, but never did. Archie wrote to her for about a year before finally admitting that he already had a wife when he married her. Ivy's reaction was to immediately institute divorce proceedings through a Canadian lawyer. It is not clear why she bothered to get a divorce when the marriage was obviously invalid.

Archie worked with a survey party during the summer of 1919. One of his fellow surveyors described Archie as "taciturn and morose with a violent, almost maniacal temper." He said Archie would sit by the camp fire at night "tapping on a dish-pan in a dull, monotonous beat, singing ancient Indian songs...that none of our Cree or Ojibwa Indians had ever heard."

The people of Bisco found that Archie was embittered by his injured foot. One man described Archie as a perfect gentleman and wonderful conversationalist when sober, but, he added, no one wanted anything to do with Archie when he was drinking. Another said that he often threatened people with violence, but it was easy to call his bluff. "If you said 'boo' to him, he ran away like a scared deer."

"[I] quickly resented any infringement on what I considered to be my personal freedom," Archie admitted, noting that his army service had intensified this trait. The war had convinced him "of the utter futility of civilization."

The war wasn't the only source of Archie's bitterness. The population of Bisco and the surrounding area had doubled since before the war. Many of the newcomers were engaged in the timber trade, and Archie was upset about the effects of large-scale logging. He said that such logging had changed what had been a Garden of Eden when he first arrived in Bisco to a place that now looked as if a drunken party had taken place.

Part of Archie's job as a ranger was to make sure the loggers had valid licences. Not surprisingly, he had several dangerous confrontations with loggers in which they drew guns and he pulled his knife. He plainly showed his disapproval of what they were doing, even if they were doing it legally. There is no record that anyone was seriously injured, but Archie's employers would not have been happy about his behaviour.

Archie's dislike of authority and desire to shock sometimes caused him to offend the religious sensibilities of his neighbours. A man named Ralph Bice told a story about Archie disrupting a Sunday morning church service by shooting at the church bell to make it ring. "We knew he was only having his own sort of fun, but it was enough for the local residents to send for the police and force Archie to take a self-imposed exile into the woods until everything cooled off."

Although Archie abandoned his own children, he was good with other people's. He bought them treats and played tricks on them. The daughter of some friends said, "Archie was one of the nicest things that happened to me when I was growing up."

A friend described a typical evening's entertainment for Archie and his friends. First they met the train and then wandered over to the store to visit. Sooner or later someone invited the gang to share a barrel of moonshine, and then they might plan an elaborate practical joke. One joke that Archie and a man named Bill Draper planned cost Archie $40. The men were sitting around at Legace's boarding house one hot summer night when Bill told Archie that he had a jug of whiskey stored in a tool box at the home of an absent friend named Ernie. Bill asked Archie if he would go and get the jug, and Archie agreed.

As Archie was leaving, Bill called out, "Better put on your snowshoes and take your axe in case Ernie's out and he has locked his front door." The next thing the men heard was a tremendous crash and Matilda Legace's scream as Archie glissaded down the boarding house stairs wearing his snowshoes and waving an axe. Half an hour later Archie returned, still wearing his snowshoes and triumphantly carrying the jug of whiskey.

Early the next morning, Bill was awakened by an indignant Ernie who had returned home late the night before to find his front door and his tool box both smashed to bits. Ernie's next-door neighbour told him that Archie had done the deed on orders from Bill.

Archie returned to his pre-war job as a ranger in the Mississauga Forest Reserve during the summers of 1920 and 1921, and he was promoted to deputy ranger. At first he was stiff and awkward, but within a few weeks he had regained his skills as a first-class canoeist. He was at his best out in the woods, where he rarely or never drank. The college students that Archie supervised over those two summers spoke well of him. They said he was a well-trained, energetic, and fair man who expected his men to work hard and carefully.

During the early 1920s Archie lived for several years with an Ojibwa family named Espaniel. They apparently took him in out of concern when they saw him drinking heavily and getting into trouble. Alex Espaniel became the father Archie never had, Annie Espaniel mothered him, and two of their six children (Jim and Jane) became his lifelong friends. From the Espaniels, Archie learned much about conservation or "the Indian way of doing things." He learned that he must keep track of the number of beaver lodges in his hunting territory, the ages of their inhabitants, and, most importantly, leave behind a pair of beavers in each lodge. On one occasion when Archie dynamited a beaver lodge, Alex was furious. Alex said he would have nothing more to do with Archie if he ever did such a thing again.

In the years immediately after the war Archie consciously changed his appearance. He had previously worn his hair long, but now he asked Jane Espaniel to help him dye it. He darkened his skin with henna and practiced forming his features into what he believed was a stern "Indian" look.

During the 1920s Archie introduced war dances to Bisco. These dances had nothing at all to do with Ojibwa or Cree traditions but rather were inspired by Archie's childhood reading. Some of the local people thought Archie's dances were fun and took part. Others strongly disapproved. When he asked Annie Espaniel to sew costumes for his first dance, she thought the idea was rather silly but agreed to do so. The Sudbury *Star* (May 30, 1923) carried a story about the dance Archie organized for Victoria Day. The dance started at 8 p.m. following the afternoon's sporting events. One man was tied to a pole as the prisoner and the others danced around him, brandishing knives or axes. Archie, as the chief, beat a drum and sang.

Archie spent the summer of 1925 guiding in the Temagami area. During that time he regularly stayed with Angele and their daughter Agnes, who was now 14. Angele made him a new leather outfit, and she became pregnant with their second child, a daughter named Flora. After that summer, Archie never saw either Angele or Agnes again, and he never met Flora.

Chapter 4
Pony

 t was in the summer of 1925 that a young Mohawk woman named Gertrude Bernard saw Archie Belaney for the first time. She sat reading under the pines near the dock at the Wabikon Resort on Temagami Island and looked up when she heard the gritting sound of someone beaching a canoe. She was later to write, "I saw a man dressed in brown deerskin stepping with the speed and grace of a panther from a canoe. And there he stood, tall, straight and handsome, gazing wistfully across the lake...But what really set my imagination afire was his long hair and wide-brimmed hat...In my imagination, this man looked like the ever so thrilling hero of my youth, Jesse James... "

Pony

Archie went up to the resort office without stopping to speak to the girl who was gazing at him so avidly, and shortly afterwards returned to his canoe and paddled away. He had just been hired as a guide and knew he would have plenty of time to meet the girl that evening at supper. Although he had recently reconnected with his wife and daughter, he was definitely interested in getting to know this young beauty, who was only a little older than his daughter.

Gertrude, who was known as Pony or Gertie to family and friends and would later become famous under the name Anahareo, hurried to the office as soon as Archie was gone to find out who he was. She was not used to having men ignore her. That evening she waited where he would have to pass by her on his way to the dining room but was disillusioned when she met him. She learned that "this Godlike male, whose proud and masterful appearance struck my very soul with awe," was a big tease. "He seemed to be under the impression that the best way to win friends and influence 19-year-old girls was to be annoying."

The attraction between Archie and Pony was quick and mutual, but — due to Archie's teasing and Pony's hot temper — they quarrelled every time they met over the next few days. Then Archie went off on a four-day guiding trip. While he was gone, Pony was called home to Mattawa (a town north of Algonquin Park on the Ontario–Quebec border) because her niece had died, and she did not return to work at Wabikon following the funeral. She asked her father if she could invite

Archie to visit before she left for school in Toronto that fall, and he agreed.

She mailed the invitation and, to her shock, Archie arrived the next day — before he could possibly have received her letter. He explained his appearance with an apologetic smile, "I wrote and told you I was coming, but I guess I got on the same train, being it was there."

Archie told her that he had decided it might be prudent to leave town, as the police were after him for slugging the station agent in Bisco. The agent had failed to deliver a telegram offering Archie a guiding job. Pony later admitted, "I loved this and was enthusiastic at the prospect of more blood and thunder."

Archie noticed her excitement and added sarcastically, "I'm sorry I didn't kill the guy because I know how much you would have enjoyed that."

He went on to tell Pony how he had accidentally cut a man with a knife on a previous occasion. He said the police had initially charged him with attempted murder for that incident, and they warned him that they would relay the charge if he ever got into more trouble.

According to Harry Woodsworth, Bisco's law officer, Archie's version of the story was not quite accurate. In April 1925 a warrant was issued charging Archie with being disorderly at the Biscotasing Railway Station. As Woodsworth said, "Archie had one or two drinks too many and was owl hooting at the station." It was a minor offence, and Archie didn't leave town until three months later, Woodsworth recalled.

Archie got along so well with Pony's father that she felt ignored after supper and went to spend the night with her cousin. The next morning she arrived home to find that Archie was leaving, angry that she had gone to her cousin's without telling him. She couldn't convince him to stay longer, but when he left her he said, "I'll be seeing you whether you like it or not."

Every day for two weeks after that, Archie wrote a letter to Pony, and some were as long as 90 or 100 pages. The letters were followed by five months of silence. Finally Pony wrote and told Archie she would not be going to school in Toronto until the next semester. He responded by sending her a train ticket to visit him at Forsythe in northern Quebec where he was trapping that winter because Ontario had passed a law prohibiting non-natives from trapping in the province.

Pony's father agreed to her going for a week's visit. She arrived at Forsythe after a 38-hour train trip and was "dumped off, as it were, into a snowbank" in the dark. The entire population of Forsythe consisted of four families of railway maintenance workers. Three of the houses were in darkness. At the fourth, Archie introduced her to the railway foreman, Mr. Henri, and his family. She was to board with the Henris during her visit. The rest of the community and three trappers from the area were all at the Henri house to greet her. After supper, they danced until morning to an orchestra consisting of a fiddle, guitar, and accordion. The next night there was a similar party at another house.

About 4 a.m. on the second night, they returned to the Henris' house. After "a lively post-mortem" on the party, the family went to bed, leaving Archie and Pony alone for the first time since Pony's arrival. She commented that she would hate to leave Forsythe the next day because she had enjoyed herself so much. Archie replied that he wouldn't be sorry to leave "because I've been away from my traps too long as it is."

Pony was shocked and angry. She indignantly retorted that she was sorry to have overstayed her welcome. After some angry whispered accusations back and forth, Archie finally made her understand that he had meant for her to spend several days visiting his trapping grounds and didn't consider her stay in Forsythe as part of her visit with him. She wrote to her father that she was going into the bush for a week.

Archie had arranged for a dog team to take Pony in to his camp, but the man didn't show up. Pony agreed to snow-shoe in when Archie told her it was not a long trip and they would take it easy. Pony, who had done little or no snow-shoeing before, didn't discover until they were well underway that the camp was 25 kilometres away. After five hours without a break, she was exhausted. Archie finally stopped, saying they were half-way there and it was time for lunch. He knocked the snow off a fallen tree and invited her to sit down. Then he handed her a slice of frozen bannock and told her to put some snow on it. "It keeps the sugar from sliding off," he said as he passed her some sugar.

It was long after dark before Archie finally said, "We're home. Welcome to Sunset Lodge." Pony could see nothing except a mound of snow with the top of a tent and a stove pipe stuck in it. Archie began shovelling with one of his snowshoes. Suddenly he disappeared. Then a light appeared in a small hole and he called to her to come in. She crawled through the opening, and would have dropped four feet to the ground if he hadn't caught her. She collapsed onto the bunk and was instantly asleep.

Some time later Archie woke her to offer tea. Now she had a better look at her surroundings. The tent she had seen from outside formed a roof over log walls. The white canvas was mildewed and grey with age, and the walls were windowless. The floor and the table were both made of rough poles, but Archie had made a fire in the tiny tin box stove, so the place was warm.

Archie served moose meat and raisin pancakes for supper. When Pony acted coolly polite during the meal, Archie apologized for the way he had behaved on the trip. He said he was putting her to the test, which made her even angrier.

After supper Archie took Pony back outside, saying he had a surprise for her. There, she saw a cabin in the moonlight. Over the door was a sign painted in black canoe pitch. It said "Pony Hall." Her anger evaporated. She was even more delighted when she saw the inside of the cabin. The log walls, still covered in green bark and chinked with moss in reds, greens, and yellows, looked like tapestry. There was a table covered with new oilcloth, a moose-hide rug, a stove, and a bunk piled high with balsam boughs and covered with a red Hudson's Bay blanket.

Pony's delight turned to shock when Archie said that he would have to leave the next day to see to his traps. He would be gone for a few days, he told her. Having been raised in town, Pony was horrified. "You can't leave me here alone. I've never been in the bush by myself before," she confessed.

When Archie expressed surprise that she was afraid to be alone, she quickly backtracked. "Oh, I'm not scared. Never think that. I was only thinking what a queer way to treat a guest."

Archie pretended to believe her. "That's the stuff. I knew all along that you weren't afraid. I'm sorry I mentioned it."

Archie became serious long enough to give Pony a crash course on how to look after herself while he was gone. First, he showed her how to care for the water hole, impressing upon her how important it was not to allow it to freeze over. Making a new water hole was not easy, he told her, but it was easier than chipping out an old one that had frozen over. He instructed her to cover the hole with at least 46 centimetres (18 inches) of snow after each use, and to mark the spot with the ice chisel. She was surprised that dumping snow into the water hole would keep it from freezing, but he assured her it would. He said it would not be difficult to scoop out the snow when next she needed to get water.

To make a new hole, Pony would first have to shovel one

or two metres of snow off the ice. Then she would have to chop through more than a metre of ice, first using an axe and then switching to an ice chisel attached to a long pole. Because the chisel blade was only five centimetres wide, the whole process would take a very long time.

Next, Archie said he wanted to show her the bear's den. He led her to a lean-to in the bush. He struck a match and Pony peered in fearfully. "I guess he hasn't come yet," Archie said, reaching in and handing her a roll of toilet paper. "I'm using this for bait," he went on, immensely enjoying his little joke.

Then Archie quickly became serious again. He told Pony she should never leave the cabin except when she had to get wood and water or use the toilet, and that she must not go out without her snowshoes. She was to be extremely careful when using the axe, when making up the fire, or handling the lighted lamp.

To drive home the lesson, Archie told Pony how a moment's carelessness had almost cost him his life earlier that winter. Trappers used strychnine to kill wolves and foxes at that time, and one night Archie put a package of strychnine in his grub box. He removed the strychnine the next day and promptly forgot what he had done. After he returned home and was repacking his grub box for his next trip, he noticed some white powder spilled in the bottom of the box. Thinking it was sugar, he carefully poured it into the sugar bowl. Shortly after putting sugar in his tea the next morning, he felt as though someone had slugged him across the back of the head with a sack of flour. He immediately remembered the strychnine.

He told Pony that the treatment for strychnine poisoning was mustard to cause vomiting, followed by milk as an antidote. He dumped dry mustard into another cup of tea and drank it down. Then he grabbed a can of milk, which was frozen solid, and put it in the stove. The mustard acted. He then took the can of milk out of the stove before it exploded, opened it, and drank some before collapsing on his bunk. He recovered without receiving medical treatment. According to current information on strychnine poisoning, you should neither induce vomiting nor drink fluids but rather go to a hospital immediately.

When it was almost time for Pony to return home, Archie said he had to make an overnight trip to check more traps before taking her to catch the train. She persuaded him to take her along. In early afternoon they found the first trap with an animal in it — a marten. Pony felt sick when Archie clubbed it to death with the axe handle. She later wrote about this experience: "For the rest of the day I could hardly put one snowshoe before the other. I felt as if I were carrying a ton...I was depressed, angry, and disgusted. Before the afternoon was over Archie picked up another marten and two lynx; but, thank goodness, they were dead when we came to them."

Until Archie announced that it was time to stop for the night, Pony hadn't realized that they would be sleeping outdoors. Archie began digging a hole with one of his snow-shoes, making a pit large enough to hold two beds, the grub box, and a fire. He instructed her to pack down the excavated snow to form a six-foot wall around the pit. Then he spread the tarpaulin from the toboggan over it to form a roof. Pony was surprised at how comfortable it was once they had a carpet of boughs to sleep on and a fire going.

Making a fire in the deep snow was a major undertaking. They first had to make a platform of green logs. Otherwise, "the fire would melt itself out of sight before the tea was made."

At the end of her first week Pony decided to stay on for a second week. And by the time they got to Forsythe for Easter, Pony had been away from home for nearly two months.

Five letters from Pony's father were waiting for her. He told her not to come home unless she was married. Then, when she went to make her Easter confession, the priest wouldn't give her absolution. Pony was indignant.

It's hard to believe that, at age 19, Pony could not understand why her father and the priest were upset with her. Until very recently, couples who lived together before marriage were almost certain to create a scandal. But Pony wrote in her book that she didn't realize what the problem was until some time later. She said she had lived in Pony Hall while Archie stayed in his shabby tent cabin.

Pony was born at Mattawa, Ontario, in 1906, and had always lived in town until she met Archie. Like Archie, she had had a difficult childhood. Pony was four when her mother died and she went to live with an aunt who did not treat her very well. Finally she told her father what was happening and he brought her back home. Pony's grandmother, who lived to be 108, taught Pony many traditional native women's skills such as tanning hides, sewing, and doing beadwork. Pony was a very accomplished needle-woman.

Because of her father's letters, Pony decided to stay with Archie for the spring trapping season rather than return home. At the end of the season, they went to the village of Doucet to sell Archie's winter catch and pay off his grubstake. There was a dance that night, but Pony did not enjoy herself because many people gave her the cold shoulder. "Who could blame them?" she later admitted. "But at the time, I did."

Pony also felt that Archie, who kept busy playing the piano, was ignoring her. She angrily went up to her room and ordered a bottle of whiskey. The next day she felt so ashamed that she decided to leave town. Archie told her she could not go, and they quarrelled. He insisted that they should either get married or she should return to her father. She said she would do neither and, in a fit of rage, she pulled his hunting knife from his belt and cut his arm. As Archie's arm became covered in blood, she went into hysterics. He finally managed to calm her down and get her back to her room.

Pony spent the next three days locked in her room. Archie knocked on the door several times, but she refused to talk to him. When at last she broke down and admitted for the first time that she loved him, they made plans to get married the next day.

But fate was to intervene. An Ojibwa from Lac Simon (some 70 kilometres west) arrived the next day to ask Archie for help in defending two band members in court. They had been charged with destroying gear and burning down a cabin that belonged to some trappers. The men said they had done so because the trappers had not picked up their unused strychnine baits the previous year, and the band lost many of their dogs as a result. Archie agreed to plead their case in court and successfully argued that the trappers had broken the law first. As a result, the two Ojibwa men were sentenced to only 30 days in jail instead of the usual sentence of two years.

Archie took Pony to visit at Lac Simon before he went off to work as a fire ranger for the summer, and while they were there the chief blessed their marriage. Pony was 20 and Archie was 38. Only a couple of months previously Pony had been concerned about getting to Forsythe to celebrate Easter. As a Catholic she felt obligated to make her "Easter Duty" by going to confession and attending Mass. Now she willingly entered into a traditional native marriage without benefit of clergy. She had been deeply offended by the priest who refused absolution, and she was madly in love. Also, she must have realized that she couldn't marry Archie in a Catholic ceremony while Angele was living.

Archie told Pony about his previous relationships with Angele, Marie, and Ivy. This was one of the few times he didn't try to deceive a woman he was interested in. When Pony asked if he had left Angele because she was a bad wife, he admitted that it was his selfishness rather than anything Angele had done or not done. "When I discovered that I didn't like marriage, I dropped it like a hot potato."

But he almost immediately backtracked, hinting that Angele may have been "wild" and that Agnes was not his daughter. He also said he believed the marriage was invalid because the officiating clergyman was an American.

There is no evidence to support any of this. It seems to be just another example of Archie's now ingrained habit of deception. He not only deceived others but also tried to deceive himself. At any rate, Pony seemed relatively unconcerned about Archie's previous women and found his stories about them "interesting."

Archie's account of their courtship and marriage was considerably briefer than Pony's: "The affair was quite wanting in the vicissitudes…that are said to usually beset the path of high romance. The course of true love ran exasperatingly smooth; I sent the lady a railway ticket, she came…and we were married, precisely according to plan."

Because fire rangers were not allowed to take their wives along while they were working, Archie and Pony decided that she would work at Rouyn in northern Quebec for the summer. Pony went to Rouyn but almost immediately returned because she was homesick. She convinced the chief ranger to break the rules for her and spent the rest of the summer with Archie, who was working in a fire tower that year as opposed to patrolling an area by canoe.

There was just one problem. Archie had a fear of heights amounting almost to a phobia. It took all the willpower he possessed to climb the 30 to 35-metre tower. He also hated being confined to the tiny cubbyhole at the top.

In the fall the couple returned to Doucet to pick up their winter gear and grubstake. Then they set off by canoe to the Jumping Caribou area. It was Pony's first long canoe trip, and she had a lot to learn about canoeing. Instead of keeping her paddle strokes in perfect unison with Archie's, the very talkative Pony frequently let her paddle drag in the water as she turned around to make conversation. Finally Archie had had enough. He told her that if she couldn't keep time with his paddle she would have to sit in the bottom of the canoe instead of paddling. Pony, who really wanted to do her share of the work, tried to do better.

She got into more serious trouble when they reached the first portage. Archie, who "abhorred the sight of a woman doing a man's job," did not want Pony to help portage. When he handed her an axe and the tea pail to carry and gave her what she felt was a condescending smile, Pony's famous hot temper got the better of her good judgement yet again.

She launched the canoe and headed for the centre of the river. By the time she realized she was in serious danger, it was too late to pull back. The canoe "jerked viciously" towards the foaming water below, and there seemed to be hundreds of jagged rocks poking through the water. The next thing she knew, Pony was safely at the foot of the rapids, circling dizzily in an eddy. She was so light (under 50 kilograms) that the canoe had floated down the rapids like a chip. Had she been heavier, she very likely would have drowned.

Although he sometimes found her exasperating, Archie admired Pony's ability to fit into wilderness life. He quickly learned that he was married "to no butterfly." Pony could set up camp and make portages quickly and competently, "even if she did have to sit down and powder her nose at the other end of the portage." Despite this, he was opposed to her accompanying him when he went to check on his traps. "I can't watch a trap and watch you too," he said. "And if I didn't watch you, you'd fall through the ice and take me with you, or land us in some jam that would mean the death of one or both of us."

These words proved prophetic when Pony decided to follow him one day. She caught up to him when he stopped to check a trap. He greeted her gruffly and told her that now she was there she would have to keep quiet and follow instructions. She did so, though she found it difficult to watch him put several injured animals to death.

On their return trip, Archie went out to test the ice in a small bay. Pony disobeyed his instructions to stay well back from him when they were crossing ice. The next thing she

Archie (left) and Pony (right) flanking
Sir Charles G. D. Roberts who visited in 1931

knew she was in icy water to her waist. Archie dropped to the
ice and crawled forward until she could grasp the end of an
iron-shod staff that he always carried. Once she was on
shore, Archie ordered her to head as quickly as possible back

to the cabin, about a kilometre away, stopping for nothing.

Soon her clothes were frozen stiff, and with every movement she made she felt as if she were being cut with knives. She reached the cabin safely, but it was freezing cold as the fire had gone out. She crept under the covers and waited for Archie who made up the fire before gently tending her cuts and abrasions.

After this episode Archie agreed that Pony could go out with him and learn how to trap. She soon regretted it, though, and by spring she had vowed that she would never trap again. She hated killing animals and felt that being remorseful about it did not right the wrong. "I can still hear the screams of the suffering animals — the mink, marten, fisher, lynx," she wrote. "I still see the poisoned foxes and wolves…and the drowned beaver and otter at the bottom of the lakes and streams."

That winter Archie received a rare letter from his mother. She told him that his half-brother, Leonard Scott-Brown, wanted to join the Hudson's Bay Company. When Archie wrote back to give Leonard some information, Kitty found the letter "so poetic" that she sent it to a British magazine, *Country Life.* The magazine accepted the letter for publication but did not do so until a year later (March 2, 1929).

In the article, Archie described northern Ontario as a land of "shadows and hidden trails, lost rivers and unknown lakes, a region of soft-footed creatures going their noiseless ways over the carpet of moss [where] there is silence, intense, absolute and all-embracing. It is as though one walked on the bottom of a mighty ocean of silence." He also talked about how the genuine trapper (as opposed to the man out for a quick fortune) is "as much a part of the woods as the animals themselves."

Trapping was poor in the winter of 1927–28, and world fur prices were dropping. Archie and Pony received only $600 for their winter's catch, hardly enough to pay their grubstake debt let alone provide money for the summer. So Archie decided to return to the spring hunt to earn more money, even though beavers are not normally trapped in spring because the fur is not in prime condition and the females are usually pregnant.

When the spring hunt was over, Archie asked Pony if she would like to go with him to pick up the last of their traps. She said yes.

Chapter 5
McGinnis and McGinty

hile collecting their traps at the end of the 1928 season, Archie and Pony discovered that a beaver had cut the anchor line of one of the traps and dragged it away. They couldn't locate her body, but they did find her two babies. Pony immediately fell in love with the beaver kittens and wanted to keep them, but Archie pointed out that they could sell them for $10 apiece, and they badly needed the money. There was a good market for live beavers since someone in eastern Quebec had started a beaver farm.

Archie and Pony took the kittens home and continued to argue until they were interrupted by cries from the hungry kittens, who were standing on their hind legs with their front paws raised like toddlers asking to be taken out of their cribs. They decided to give them some sweetened condensed milk but found it impossible to feed them with a spoon or bottle because neither would reach the "true" mouth. Beavers have two mouths, an outer one that covers their long, chisel-like teeth and an inner or true mouth.

Then Archie got an idea. He dipped a long stick into the thick, sticky milk and poked the stick into the beaver's mouth while Pony held it open. The kittens quickly learned to suck the milk from a stick.

The following day, when Archie and Pony were ready to set off for Doucet, they discovered one kitten was missing. They searched all day. When it was nearly dark, Pony heard Archie calling, "I've got him. I've got him." Pony found Archie buried almost to his neck in muskeg. He was gripping a branch of a willow tree with one hand and the missing beaver with the other. "Hurry, hurry," Archie yelled. "He's slipping from my grip."

Muskegs (bogs) can be virtually bottomless. Pony, terrified that Archie might lose his grip and drown, grabbed him by the wrist. Finally he convinced her that he would be fine if she would just take the beaver. A few minutes later Archie, covered with smelly black muck, was safely back on firm ground. Pony thought he would be angry, but he just shook his head and gave her a sheepish grin.

By the time they arrived at Doucet, the beaver kittens had worked their way into Archie's heart. He agreed not to sell them. In *Pilgrims of the Wild*, he described the childlike behaviour of young beavers that so touched him. "Their little sneezes and childish coughs, their little whimpers and small appealing noises of affection, their instant and pathetically eager response to any kindness, their tiny clinging hand-like forepaws, their sometimes impatiently stamping feet, and their little bursts of independence..."

Pony, who had almost given up hope of having a baby, now found herself the mother of twins. She found that "minus the diaper routine, their needs were no different than that of an infant." Sometimes she thought washing diapers might have been easier. Because beavers can only go to the toilet when they are in water, the water in their bath tub had to be changed frequently; and hauling the necessary pails of water up from the lake was hard work.

At first they referred to the beavers simply as the two Micks (short for Ahmik, the Ojibwa word for beaver), but soon they decided that each beaver needed a separate name. Because Mick was also a common nickname for an Irishman and the little beavers busily constructing their house reminded Archie of Irish railway construction workers, he decided to call them McGinty and McGinnis. As he put it, the Micks were "as energetic and at times as peppery as any two gentlemen from Cork." McGinty was also the name of a character in two comic Irish songs, "Down Went McGinty" and "Who Threw the Overalls in Mistress Murphy's Chowder?"

One day near the end of McGinnis and McGinty's first

summer, Archie suddenly announced he was through with hunting beavers. "I am now the president, treasurer, and sole member of the Society of the Beaver People," he told Pony. His dream was to help to repopulate the country with beavers, although he realized it would not be easy. First, they had to find an alternate source of income, and then they had to find a safe place to raise the beavers.

Archie didn't decide to give up trapping beavers only to please Pony. He could see the handwriting on the wall, and he knew his trapping days were numbered. Beavers were becoming scarce, prices were down, his health was not good, and Quebec (like Ontario) would likely soon ban non-native peoples from trapping beaver.

Archie had also come to feel that trapping beavers was wrong. In *Pilgrims of the Wild* he wrote about how he gradually came to see them in a different light, saying they were "like little folk from some other planet, whose language we could not yet quite understand." He decided to study beavers and attempt to prevent their extinction.

That summer Archie met a Mi'kmaq from New Brunswick who suggested that an area along the Quebec– New Brunswick border would be a perfect place to raise beavers while trapping other fur-bearing animals to earn a living. On the strength of this recommendation, Archie and Pony travelled by train to the French-Canadian community of Cabano, east of Rivière-du-Loup, near the border with New Brunswick.

While at Cabano, McGinnis and McGinty both suffered from a severe skin rash. Like anxious parents, Archie and Pony took them to the local doctor. The doctor suggested feeding them baby cereal (Pablum) if they weren't yet ready to eat the natural diet of adult beavers (mainly tree bark and water plants), and he prescribed an ointment for the rash. When Archie admitted that they were broke, the doctor refused payment.

The storekeeper was equally generous when they went to buy the Pablum and did not have 75 cents to pay for it. They asked if they could get a grubstake for their winter's trapping, and the merchant allowed them $150 worth of provisions in addition to the Pablum. The little beavers began to recover almost immediately although it took some time before their fur coats grew back in.

After this warm welcome to Cabano, Archie and Pony received some bad news — the man who had suggested the area was a trappers' paradise had been lying. In fact, the area was completely cut over by lumbermen. The locals suggested that they go north to an area called Birch Lake.

The river at Cabano was too low and swift-flowing for their heavily laden canoe to navigate. They had to hire someone to haul their supplies and gear another 25 kilometres by road with horses and a wagon while they travelled by canoe with the beavers. Archie raised the $10 to pay the teamster by capturing and selling a red fox that swam across the bow of their canoe. He said afterwards, "It seemed somehow like a betrayal. He had been free like us, and the money no sooner changed hands than I wished I had killed the poor beast outright and sold the hide instead."

When the beavers outgrew their first tin-lined travel box, Archie got the idea of transporting them in the stove, which was little more than an oblong tin box with a door for wood and a hole for the stovepipe. The beavers were allowed their freedom at night, but each morning they would obediently enter the stove for the day after it was cold and the ashes were knocked out of it.

It was now well into autumn. There had been several heavy snowfalls and the water was beginning to freeze. Because the river was so low Archie was poling the canoe, so he had to stand rather than kneel or sit as when paddling. Both the canoe and the steel-shod pole quickly became coated with ice, and it was almost impossible for him to keep his footing. One day he slipped and fell into the river. The canoe swung sideways out of control and filled with water. Within seconds both Archie and Pony were standing upright in the icy rushing river. They groped frantically for the stove, plunging their arms into the water to the shoulder in order to touch the river bottom. "Then suddenly we were holding up the dripping stove between us, although we could never remember the act of finding it," Archie wrote.

While Pony retrieved their packs, Archie salvaged the canoe, which fortunately had only suffered minor damage. Only then could they make a fire to warm and dry themselves and the beavers, whose coats were still very sparse. When they took stock afterwards they found they had lost nothing but their tea pail and a package of lard. Even two panes of window glass for their new cabin, which were tied to a washboard, were unbroken.

The next day they arrived at the stream leading to Birch Lake, where the freighter had left their cache of goods. The lake was only about five or six kilometres away. The problem was that the creek was only about a metre wide and a few centimetres deep. They would have to carry 300 kilograms of food and gear, including the canoe, overland to the lake. Even worse, the countryside was obstructed with fallen trees, marshy areas, and dense brush. Also, although there was snow, the heavy loads they had to carry and the roughness of the country prevented them from using snowshoes.

It took them two weeks to complete the nightmare trip to Birch Lake. The going was so difficult that some days they travelled less than a kilometre. Making camp each evening in the snow was an ordeal. Snow on their tent melted when they made a fire. The tent then froze stiff, making repacking it almost impossible. They ate little but frozen food. A whole winter's supply of potatoes froze and had to be thrown away.

Archie could joke about that later: "Well, that was about two hundred pounds that we didn't have to carry any more. We got considerable consolation from figuring how this helped us. Allowing five more days to get [to Birch Lake], at the rate of two hundred pounds a day saved, we had made a net gain of a thousand pounds...In the woods a man has often to turn reverses to what good account he may, but this was the first time that I had ever figured myself out of trouble by means of arithmetic."

They finally arrived at Birch Lake in the second week of November and built a cabin in a magnificent grove of birch and pine. Building the cabin took 11 days of hard work. The spaces between the logs had not yet been chinked when they moved in, so the cabin was initially no warmer than the tent. Archie arranged frozen blocks of moss around the stove to thaw out overnight so he could chink the walls the next day.

But the next morning Archie and Pony were astonished to discover the job was already underway. During the night the beavers had taken some of the thawed moss and "made a very passable attempt to chink the crevices as high as they could reach along one of the walls." The beavers were acting according to instinct — they always plug up any air leaks in their lodges.

In *The Men of the Last Frontier* Archie described what it was like to share a home with a pair of beavers.

...their activities have much the same effect on the camp that two small animated sawmills running loose would have... [They] take large slices out of table legs and chairs, and nice long splinters out of the walls...After 'lights out' the more serious work commences, such as the removal of deerskin rugs, the transferring of firewood from behind the stove into the

middle of the floor, or the improvement of some water-proof footwear by the addition of a little open-work on the soles.

He also described how beavers sharpen their teeth with the help of a longitudinal slot in their skull. This slot allows for the necessary motion of the jaws to grind their teeth together. Because this action is much like the whetting of an axe, the sound of an axe or knife being filed always filled McGinnis and McGinty with terror. They would drop everything and run to Archie or Pony for protection, evidently thinking the noise came from some large animal sharpening its teeth.

McGinty almost lost her life a third time that winter when she poisoned herself by eating some tobacco. Archie recalled hearing about a treatment for opium poisoning, and they decided to try it on McGinty. He told Pony to massage McGinty hard over her whole body and keep her awake at all costs while he prepared a mustard bath. Soaking in the bath seemed to increase McGinty's heart rate and cause her to regain consciousness. They continued alternating these treatments for more than 10 hours. McGinty had four convulsions during this time, and more than once they thought she was gone. But at last she sat up and attempted to comb out her bedraggled coat. She was out of danger.

Since there were few animals to trap around Birch Lake that winter, Archie spent most of his time writing. Although their only income was his army disability pension of $15 a month, Archie and Pony celebrated Christmas in style. He went to town and bought toys and candy for the two Micks as if they were human children. They put up a Christmas tree and decorated it with dried fruit, candy, bannock, and macaroni for the beavers. Archie made a traditional English Christmas pudding, using moose suet instead of beef suet.

That spring (1929) McGinnis and McGinty were almost a year old. In the wild, a year-old male begins to wander while a female of that age helps her mother prepare for the birth of another litter. The Micks built themselves a small beaver house where there was a bit of open water. They would remain outdoors most of the night but at daybreak would scratch at the cabin door to be let back inside. After sleeping until about noon, they would again scamper off to the "big doings outside."

When Archie and Pony went out for the mail in March, they found a cheque from *Country Life* for the article Archie's mother had sent to the magazine the previous winter. The editor also asked for more articles. Archie and Pony were jubilant. Now it seemed they had solved their money problems, and they had a good start for their beaver colony.

But their happiness quickly changed to sorrow when they got home. Dave Whitestone, a friend of Pony's father, had arrived while they were gone. He knew McGinnis and McGinty were pets, but he didn't know that Archie had given up trapping and was planning to establish a beaver colony at

Birch Lake. So Dave proudly showed them a pile of beaver pelts in the corner of the cabin. Thinking he was being helpful, he had trapped all the beavers in the lake, except McGinnis and McGinty.

Pony and Archie didn't blame Dave, but they were devastated. They couldn't bear to stay at Birch Lake any longer and returned to the Cabano area, where they set up camp on a nearby lake.

McGinnis and McGinty excitedly examined a big abandoned beaver house on the lake. As Archie and Pony watched them they wished the beavers were small again. That evening, as Archie described it, "… in answer to a call, a long clear note came back to us, followed by another in a different key. And the two voices blended and intermingled like a part song…And that long wailing cry from out the darkness was the last sound we ever heard them make. We never saw them any more."

Pony and Archie felt as if they had lost their children. Even Dave commented, seemingly in surprise, "You know I kinda like to see beaver around here myself, some way."

Chapter 6
Grey Owl Emerges

ony and Archie resigned themselves to the fact that the two young beavers, McGinnis and McGinty, were gone forever. Their friend Dave soon located another pair of young beavers, and he and Pony hiked 15 kilometres through the bush to get them. Archie had to remain in camp, as his foot had swollen up so badly (a legacy of his war wound) that he could not put any weight on it for more than a month. One beaver lived for only a few weeks. The other, named Jelly Roll, survived. She was to become the most famous beaver in the world.

When Archie's foot healed, they headed to Métis Beach, a resort on the south shore of the St. Lawrence River where Archie hoped to get a guiding job for the summer. No jobs

Grey Owl feeding a baby beaver at
Riding National Park, Manitoba in 1931

were available, so he worked as a gardener's helper. Pony also looked for work, even answering an ad for a Scandinavian maid. It turned out that Mrs. Madeline Peck, the woman who had placed the ad, already had a Scandinavian maid, who was homesick. Mrs. Peck was looking for someone who spoke the same language to visit her maid.

Mrs. Peck was such a sympathetic person that Pony told her all about the article Archie had written and about their plans to preserve the beaver. Mrs. Peck was so impressed that she asked Archie to give a lecture based on the article. Archie refused at first, but she ignored his protests. He eventually gave in after Mrs. Peck told him she had already rented the best hotel ballroom in town and sold tickets. In effect, she offered him a dare. "When you said that you believed in the things you wrote, I took it for granted you would do it."

While waiting backstage before his talk, Archie commented, "I feel like a snake that has swallowed an icicle — chilled from one end to the other." Despite his nerves, the talk was a great success. Mrs. Peck presented him with over $700 from ticket sales.

As a result of this success, Archie was asked to give other talks in the area and to teach a Scout troop about woodcraft. He demonstrated fire-making to the Scouts and told them, "When you travel in the bush, remember you must always pay attention to details. You take care of the little things, and the big things will look out for themselves."

None of the boys in the audience likely ever forgot this lesson, as shortly afterwards Archie accidentally dropped the match safe (a waterproof case for matches) that he had been showing them. It landed next to the fire and exploded. One of the boys asked innocently, "Is that one of the little things you were talking about?"

Archie and Pony returned to Cabano with over $1000 — more money than either of them had ever seen before. There was a letter waiting from *Country Life* asking Archie to write a book. Pony wanted to be a prospector, and Dave had a gold mining claim farther north that he hoped would make him enough money to retire. So Pony and Dave went prospecting while Jelly Roll and Archie settled into the cabin for the winter of 1929–30. While Pony did not leave Archie permanently until late in 1936, it was the beginning of the end of their marriage.

Archie and Jelly Roll had a relationship of equals. Archie did not consider her a pet. All Archie did for Jelly was fill her water tank daily. This was no small task, however, since it entailed making five trips to the water hole each day. Jelly got her own food and brought it into the cabin. In the wild she would have used fresh bedding each night, but she seemed to realize this would not be practical in the cabin. Instead she spread out her bedding to air and dry every day, and then reused it. She treated the broom as sort of "staff of office," carrying it around on her tours of inspection "as self-appointed janitor" for the camp. If she got hungry, the broom straws served as a snack similar to dried breakfast cereal. Finally Archie got tired of trying to reclaim the broom and purchased a new one.

Over the winter of 1929–30, Archie worked frantically on the manuscript of his first book for *Country Life*. He so often woke from sleep with ideas for the book that he finally built a table beside his bunk so he could "jot down any notions that came along."

At this time Archie decided he could more effectively

draw attention to both the plight of the beaver and the shabby treatment accorded to Canada's native peoples if he spoke as an "Indian." Over the next two years he quite consciously established a native identity in his correspondence with the editor of *Country Life*. In a letter about the dedication for his book, he acknowledged that Mrs. Scott-Brown had first brought his work to the notice of *Country Life*. Then, in an attempt to convince the editor that he was not an educated Englishman whose proud mother had sent in his account of trapping in Canada, he referred to her as a stepmother with whom he was not well acquainted. He went on to say he wanted to dedicate his book to his aunt. "My own mother I unfortunately never knew," he wrote. "An aunt took her place, and it is to her that I must give the credit for the ordinary education that enables me to interpret into words the spirit of the forest...I would much like that tribute to her to remain, should the book itself be worth printing."

Archie now began to call himself Wa-Sha-Quon-Asin, which he translated as "Grey Owl" or "He-Who-Flies-by-Night." There are two grey-coloured owls living in northern Ontario — the great grey and the Eastern screech. Most English-speaking people would immediately think of the great grey when they heard the name Grey Owl, but in fact Wa-Sha-Quon-Asin, which translates as "white beak owl," is the Ojibwa name for the Eastern screech owl.

There is little doubt that Archie named himself for the screech owl. In *Tales of an Empty Cabin* he described "...the weird and ghoulish cachinnation of the grey owls, they of the shining beak, so called by the Indians on account of [their] white shiny beak. This bird laughs hideously in certain seasons."

Despite his chosen name, Archie wrote (in *Pilgrims of the Wild*) that the beaver, rather than owls, should have been his "patron beast." He said the owl was a "detestable bird" whose name had been given him because of his love of travelling and working at night.

In May 1929 Archie still referred to native people as "them." He claimed he had been adopted by the Ojibwa about 20 years previously. Then in November of that same year he wrote that for about 15 years "he spoke nothing but Indian." He signed his name as "Archie Grey Owl" (rather than "Archie Belaney") for the first time in November 1930. His transformation was complete when he announced that he had some "Indian blood" in February 1931 and finally declared himself an "Indian writer who writes as an Indian" in July 1931.

In his autobiographical book *Pilgrims of the Wild* (not published until 1935), Archie was inconsistent. Sometimes he referred to himself as a native. In one place he wrote, "For we are Indian, and have perhaps some queer ideas," and in another he said he was "a gloomy half-breed." Then, in describing the difficulties he and Pony had adjusting to marriage, he wrote, "I had been a most appreciative husband, not at all indifferent or inattentive as the real Indians often were."

Grey Owl Emerges

Early in the summer of 1930 Archie caught a young male beaver in a trap he had set for an otter. While trying to escape, the beaver suffered a badly broken hind foot, a gash in his head, and shattered teeth. For two weeks Archie worked at saving the beaver's foot. He was successful, but he gave some of the credit to "the antiseptic effect of the leeches which clustered in the wound on his subsequent return to natural conditions." Archie named the beaver Rawhide because of a loose piece of dried scalp that remained when his gash had healed. Although the weather was cold, Archie could not make a fire during the time he was nursing Rawhide — the beaver was terrified by the noise of the stove and even by tobacco smoke.

When Jelly Roll first saw Rawhide, she was jealous and tried to beat him up. Archie finally had to carry her down to the lake and keep the door fastened so she would not attack Rawhide again. Once Rawhide recovered from his injuries, Archie regretfully turned him loose. But the beaver had become attached to Archie and remained near the camp. Jelly continued to be jealous and repeatedly drove him away. He stubbornly continued to come back. He seemed "almost pitifully anxious" for Jelly's companionship.

One day Archie returned to camp to find Jelly lying on the ground. She was seriously wounded, and Rawhide had suffered some lesser injuries. An enormous rogue male had attacked Jelly and would undoubtedly have killed her if Rawhide had not come to her rescue. (The average full-grown beaver weighs between 15 and 22 kilograms, but a few reach twice that size.) Jelly recovered from her wounds and after that lived peacefully with Rawhide. They later became mates.

National Parks of Canada made a film about the beavers in September 1930. Archie and Pony were out canoeing when the crew arrived, and Jelly was with them. Jelly could climb into the canoe from the water without upsetting it, and she enjoyed diving off the stern seat into the water. But when the canoe was pulled up on shore, Jelly had trouble getting out of the canoe gracefully. When the film director, a man named Campbell, saw Jelly awkwardly exiting the canoe like a nervous fat lady, he shouted to his camera man, "Quick, Charlie, let's shoot."

As Charlie ran forward with his camera, Pony threw her arms around Jelly and Archie lunged at Campbell with his knife. Campbell shouted again, "Stop, you damn fool. We only want to get a picture of her." Finally, peace was established, and Campbell and Archie later became friends.

Once the movie was completed, Pony found life almost unbearable. For the talkative Pony, living with a writer was worse than being alone. She felt she had to constantly tiptoe around the cabin and check any spontaneous outbursts of conversation. When Archie said his book could not be finished until January at the earliest, she decided she could not face three or four more months of living in "this morgue-like atmosphere." She still loved him, but decided to go to work in a Quebec winter resort, with the understanding that she would return if Archie became sick or needed help with the beavers.

Archie didn't try to prevent Pony from leaving. He understood that she needed something to do and that she required more companionship than he could provide while he was writing. He once told her, "The only way I can hold you is by letting you go."

Although Archie and Pony saw the beavers as their children, these animals can be dangerous. Archie wrote that they could easily kill a dog "with one slashing bite of their razor-edged teeth, aimed always at the throat." He said domesticated beavers would not bite the people they lived with, but they would accept "neither food nor favour from strangers." After Jelly had been attacked by the rogue beaver, she would not tolerate strangers coming to the cabin unless Archie or Pony were present. One day she chased three people who came to visit. One climbed a tree to escape. On another occasion she became annoyed at a female visitor. Noticing that Jelly was about to attack, a man stepped in front of the girl to defend her. Before Archie could intervene, Jelly's sharp teeth had cut a tendon in the man's leg.

In January 1931 the beaver film was having its premiere at the Canadian Forestry Association's annual meeting in Montreal, and Archie was invited to be the guest speaker. He invited Pony to join him there. Both his speech and the film were great successes. The next day's headline in one Montreal newspaper read, "Full-blooded Indian gives lecture on Wild Life," and Archie did not set the record straight. It was also about this time that Pony became known to the public as Anahareo.

Although Archie called her Pony or Gertie in their personal life, he always referred to her as Anahareo in his speeches and writing. In *Pilgrims of the Wild* he introduced "my wife Gertrude who will be referred to from now on by her tribal name of Anahareo." Anahareo was not Pony's native or tribal name. It apparently was a name Archie made up in honour of her great-great-grandfather, a Mohawk chief named Naharrenou.

After the film premiere Archie became ill with pneumonia and spent two weeks in a Montreal hospital. Pony left her job to take care of Jelly and Rawhide for the remainder of the winter. Archie wrote to *Country Life* to tell them he was giving up the trail due to his wounded foot and the effects of gas on his lungs — and because he had tuberculosis, "the bane of our race." There is no evidence that he had tuberculosis, but he certainly did have lung problems.

At this time Lloyd Roberts, son of the famous Canadian nature writer Sir Charles G.D. Roberts, stepped in to assist Archie in his book negotiations with *Country Life*. The two men had made contact earlier, when Lloyd wrote to tell Archie how much he had enjoyed reading his articles in the Canadian Forestry Association magazine, *Forest and Outdoors*. Archie was so grateful for Lloyd's help that he invited him to visit at Cabano. Lloyd accepted the invitation and later described his visit in detail. He said that Archie and Pony lived in a one-room cabin with the marks of beaver teeth everywhere. The room was cluttered and untidy. The only furnishings were two bunks, a rough table, and a couple of chairs. Hunting gear and fishing tackle sat everywhere, along with storage bags and boxes. Two tiny beaver kitten skulls, in memory of McGinnis and McGinty, hung over one window.

Pony served a meal of bannock, bacon, beans, and molasses. Afterwards Archie squatted on the floor while Pony and Lloyd settled themselves on the two bunks. Archie began to talk, and at about midnight Pony fell asleep but Lloyd continued to listen. Archie got up occasionally to put another log in the stove, and at about 5 a.m. Archie broke off. "Ah, brother. It will soon be dawn," he said. "What about a snack?"

The two men slept until noon the next day, and they were storm-bound for the next five days. At the end of the visit Pony confided to Lloyd that she would never spend another winter in the bush. "It's all very well for Archie," she said. "His whole soul is taken up with his beaver and his writing. But I want to be doing something useful, prospecting for uranium or gold, or else driving a dog team."

Because of Archie's success at the Canadian Forestry Association meeting, he was offered a job in the spring of 1931 as "caretaker of park animals" at Riding Mountain National Park in Manitoba. The Parks commissioner wrote:

"The providing of a position for Grey Owl was entirely to serve our purpose of securing publicity for the National Parks and for wild life conservation by using Grey Owl's beaver and Grey Owl's personality as a spear-head in that connection."

So it happened that, at the beginning of the Great Depression when thousands of Canadians were unemployed, Archie found himself with a government job.

Chapter 7
A Lake Called Ajawaan

uring the winter of 1930–31 the two-year-old beavers, Jelly Roll and Rawhide, lived in a lodge under the ice. In the wild, beavers of this age leave their parents and set out on their own. Archie was worried that the pair might revert to the wild by spring so in March he and Pony began to make daily journeys out to the lodge. They talked to the beavers and offered them sapling trees through a hole in the ice. When Jelly and Rawhide finally came out of the lodge, Archie loaded them into a ventilated tin box, and set off for Manitoba by train.

Things began well at Riding Mountain. They had a beautiful log cabin to live in, and Jelly Roll had four kittens in May. Unfortunately, the summer of 1931 was the climax of a

10-year dry cycle in the area. As a result, the level of Beaver Lodge Lake became so low that it would have been impossible for the beavers to winter there. The Parks Department suggested they might find better conditions in Prince Albert National Park, some 280 kilometres northwest, in Saskatchewan.

Archie went to meet Major J.A. Wood, superintendent of the Saskatchewan park, which had been established only four years earlier. Wood told Archie that he knew of an ideal location for the beavers, a lake called Ajawaan. As soon as Archie saw Lake Ajawaan, he knew he had found the place he'd been dreaming of for so long. The lake was small but deep. It lay gleaming like a splash of quicksilver among wooded hills. The surrounding countryside was beautiful as well, and filled with wildlife. Ajawaan was accessible only by paddling and hiking 18 kilometres from the village of Waskesiu by way of Lakes Waskesiu and Kingsmere. Despite its seclusion, it was within reach of any visitor who had a genuine desire to visit Archie and his beaver family.

Archie, Pony, and the beavers moved to Lake Ajawaan at the end of October, as soon as a cabin was built and supplies portaged in. The new cabin was divided into two parts. The humans' section had a floor of adzed logs while the beavers' section had a dirt floor. A low fence divided the two, but a gateway allowed the beavers to come and go as they pleased. The most important feature of the cabin was a plunge-hole — a submerged tunnel going under the cabin's foundation out to the beavers' feed raft on the lake.

Grey Owl's cabin and the beaver lodge at Lake Ajawaan, Saskatchewan

The first month in the new cabin was difficult. Archie and Pony couldn't let the beavers use the plunge-hole until the lake froze over for fear that they would disappear. During that time, Rawhide had been "alarmed to the point of insanity" (in Pony's words) because he had no house or food for his family. He only relaxed once he discovered the plunge-hole with a supply of food at the end.

Over the winter the beavers began building a house for themselves inside the cabin, against the wall and over the plunge-hole. Poplar bark was the mainstay of their diet and peeled poplar branches were their building material, so the lodge could go up only as fast as the beavers ate. After many weeks, Rawhide completed a functioning beaver lodge and the family moved in.

Jelly Roll had been used to sleeping in Archie's bed, but once Rawhide and Jelly Roll became mates Rawhide strongly disapproved of this. If he awoke and found Jelly missing, "he would emit loud wailing noises and come over and drive her away into their cubby-hole." He was, as Archie put it, "something of a martinet" in family matters.

Archie's first book, which came out in late 1931 when he was 43 years old, was an immediate success. Entitled *The Men of the Last Frontier*, it contained a collection of stories about life on the trail, his native friends, and the animals of the wilderness. Grey Owl emerged as one of Canada's pioneer conservationists.

Believing that he had to entertain his readers as well as inform them, Archie sometimes altered the facts to make his stories more interesting or dramatic. For example, in *The Men of the Last Frontier* he wrote about being formally adopted into the Ojibwa band at Biscotasing. He said he became a "blood brother" and proudly received his Ojibwa name, Wa-Sha-Quon-Asin, in an elaborate ancient ritual that included dancing, chanting, and feasting.

Although he enjoyed a close relationship with the Espaniel family, who were members of the Bisco Ojibwa band, Jim Espaniel stated that Archie had never been adopted. Every fall before the band went to their winter trapping grounds they held a Wabeno, or thanksgiving festival, with dancing and feasting all night. Archie's story suggested that he had been adopted at a Wabeno, but Jim said that adoptions never occurred then. Jim also said that Archie had never attended the band's annual council and powwow, as the presence of non-natives was strictly forbidden.

Archie had wanted to call his book "The Vanishing Frontier" and was angry with the publishers for changing the title. He wrote to the editor: "That you changed the title shows that you…missed the entire point of the book. You still believe that man as such is pre-eminent, governs the powers of Nature. So he does, to a large extent, in civilization, but not on the Frontier…I speak of Nature, not men; they are incidental, used to illustrate a point only."

Archie also told his friend Lloyd Roberts how annoyed he was at being considered a college man now that he had written a successful book. He claimed in a letter to Roberts that anything he had accomplished in his writing was the result of observation and "a sympathetic insight into my life-long environment," not formal education. He would only acknowledge that an aunt had given him a good basic education and that civilization had been kind to him in taking his message to heart.

A daughter, Shirley Dawn, was born to Pony and Archie in August 1932. When Pony arrived home with the baby, she found their homecoming "less a reunion than it was a surprise party." The roof had been removed from their cabin, and inside she found a photographer named Bill perched atop a bunk "taking movies of a procession of beaver carrying sticks and armloads of mud across our living-room floor."

Later, the photographer continued filming outside. Suddenly Charlie, a bull moose that Archie had made friends with, came crashing down the hill. (It was mating season.) Bill ignored Charlie and kept filming. Archie decided they had better go inside because Charlie was getting too bold, but Bill paid no attention. Finally Archie yelled in desperation, "I warn you, I'll not shoot that moose to protect you."

When Bill finally understood the danger he dashed into the cabin, leaving his camera behind. Charlie tossed camera and tripod into the air with one antler and disappeared back into the bush. Archie retrieved the camera just as Jelly Roll began to drag it down to the lake.

On another occasion Archie heard a crackling noise outside and discovered Charlie walking across his canoe, which was pulled up on the beach. Archie placed the damaged canoe on a rack so he could mend it later, but he never got the chance to do so. Shortly afterwards the beavers cut down a large tree that fell across the canoe and destroyed it.

Archie continued to work long hours at his writing, and Pony and Shirley Dawn spent much of their time away from home. Archie said little about their separation. "It is now the Moon of Snowshoes," he wrote. "Anahareo and small new daughter are spending the winter out in town. The beaver are safely stowed away within their fortress...And I am lonesome for them all, and so I spend my time with them on paper."

One day Archie gave the beavers a bundle of shingles left over from roofing the cabin. The next day, when he took a visitor out to see Jelly Roll and Rawhide at work, the two men were amazed to discover that one section of the beaver lodge was neatly covered with shingles. They retired to the cabin in awestruck silence and drank quantities of very strong tea. When the visitor got up to leave, Archie asked if he didn't want to wait to see the beavers themselves. The man shook his head, saying that he had only recently got out of hospital and he didn't think he could stand another shock that day.

Actually, as Archie later explained, beavers will pick up almost any piece of wood for building purposes. They had laid the shingles on top because their oblong shape made it difficult to push them into the lodge.

Jelly and Rawhide regularly picked up a weird assortment of household articles. Some were never seen again; others were later located embedded in the surface of their lodge "like raisins in a pudding." One morning Archie even found the canoe paddles "firmly enmeshed in the structure of the house."

At least one other visitor was shocked by the beavers' behaviour. Archie rushed out one day when he heard a

Grey Owl and a friendly beaver in a canoe
on the shores of Lake Ajawaan, Saskatchewan

scream. He met a woman by the beaver dam who exclaimed, "Do you know what I have just seen? A beaver going by with a paintbrush."

When Archie looked incredulous, she added, "Oh, I know you won't believe me, but that's what I saw."

A man had been painting the roof earlier in the day, and his paintbrush was now missing. Later that evening, the paintbrush turned up again with "the fresh imprint of four very sharp incisor teeth upon it."

Because he was displeased with the *Country Life* editor who altered the title of his first book, Archie changed English publishers. His Canadian publisher, Hugh Eayrs, suggested a young Canadian named Lovat Dickson, who had just opened his own publishing company in London, England.

Dickson published Archie's second book, *Pilgrims of the Wild*, in 1935. *Pilgrims* was an autobiographical account of how Archie and Pony had stopped trapping and begun raising beavers. Archie was so elated by the positive reviews of this second book that he sent a copy to King George VI. It was acknowledged by the secretary to the Canadian Governor-General, who wrote, "His Majesty much appreciates Grey Owl's action in sending this book and is glad to have a copy of it."

Archie also sent a copy to Alex Espaniel, with the inscription, "To one whom I am proud to call 'Dad' and who taught me much of whatever I may know...From Grey Owl (Archie Belaney)."

Around that time Alex's daughter Jane met Archie and was startled to see him made up like a Plains Indian. She told him she had liked *Pilgrims* but found statements identifying him as a representative of the Ojibwa rather bizarre, since she had always known him as an Englishman. She also took exception to some of his stories. For example, although beaver kits are born with a full set of teeth, he had written,

Grey Owl

"Indian mothers, bereaved of an infant, had suckled baby beavers at their breasts and thus gained some solace."

Chapter 8
"A Single Green Leaf"

mmediately after the success of *Pilgrims of the Wild*, Lovat Dickson presented Archie with two proposals. First, he asked Archie to write a children's book, and second, he suggested that Archie give a series of lectures sponsored by Dickson's publishing company in Great Britain during the fall and early winter of 1935. Archie agreed to both proposals.

The children's book, *Sajo and the Beaver People*, is a fictionalized account of the lives of McGinnis and McGinty. A young native girl named Sajo makes pets of two beaver kittens that her hunter father brings home. Her father is later forced to sell one of the kittens in order to buy food for his family. After Sajo has a dream, she and her brother travel to the big city to try to get their beavers back from the zoo where he's been taken. The book became extremely popular, and excerpts from it appeared in Canadian school readers almost as soon as it was published.

Pony, who had been away all summer, came back home to help Archie prepare for his English tour. He presented her with five moose hides and asked her to make him a new shirt and leggings. He also gave her couple of pounds of beads and a pattern he had drawn of an elaborate beadwork design that he wanted to decorate his outfit. Pony objected, since she had only three weeks to sew the entire outfit by hand. She wouldn't have time to do fancy beadwork. Besides, she pointed out, bushmen don't wear beadwork.

Archie agreed, but said he was not going as a bushman. "I'm going as the Indian they expect me to be," he said. "Read the fan mail and the book reviews, and you'll see what I mean. And besides, in case I can't deliver the goods, I can at least give them a show for their money…I'd do anything, and I mean anything, if I thought it would make people listen to what I've got to say."

Pony finally agreed to the beadwork, which included a maple leaf on one shoulder and a white beaver on the other. She worked almost up to the hour that Archie left.

Dickson praised Archie's contributions in planning the tour, saying that he "read the English mind better than we did." Archie suggested that the tour advertising convey Grey Owl as a modern Hiawatha and an interpreter of the spirit of the wilderness. Britain, like Canada, was facing hard economic times in the 1930s, and the prevailing mood of the country was pessimism about the future. Archie offered no cure for the ills of civilization but he did offer hope. He grasped this when he told his audiences, "You are tired with years of civilization. I come to offer you — what? A single green leaf."

Dickson picked Archie up from the boat at Southampton on his arrival in England in October 1935. He drove him to London where he had booked accommodations in a gloomy hotel "stiff with the respectability of the late Victorian era." It was such a depressing place that Dickson felt guilty about leaving Archie there. When Dickson returned the next morning to take Archie to his first interview, he found him standing in the bedroom exactly where he had left him the previous night, his pack still unopened and the bed showing no signs of having been slept in. "I could not believe that he had stood there all night," Dickson later wrote, "but I had to believe it. His face was white and strained. Without any other greeting he said to me in a low tense voice, 'Get me out of here, brother.'"

Dickson assured Archie that he would find him a more comfortable hotel, but Archie replied, "I don't want another hotel. I'll bunk in with you. You've got a home, haven't you?"

Dickson, newly married, wasn't certain how his wife would react to an unexpected house guest, but he needn't have worried. "...I soon began to see," Dickson said, "that somewhere in his forest fastness this particular Indian had learnt how to handle women, and soon not only my wife, but the domestics…and even my new dog…formed a protective custody against my tendency to monopolize my find, and push him too hard."

Dickson learned that certain topics or questions annoyed Grey Owl. Being called a "Red" Indian was one. Another was attempts to photograph him with domestic animals. Most of all, he disliked questions about his past. His eyes would become cold and unfriendly, and the questioner felt the strength of his dislike.

Dickson urged Archie to throw away his formal notes and talk to the audience as if they were guests around the camp fire at Lake Ajawaan. Within a week, his natural humour broke through, and roars of laughter from the audience regularly punctuated his lectures.

Archie later recalled, "When I stood on those platforms I did not need to think. I merely spoke of the life and the animals I had known all my days. I was only the mouth, but nature was speaking."

Although he shared his home with Archie for a month or more, Dickson never suspected that Archie was not who he said he was. In a magazine article entitled "Grey Owl, Man of the Wilderness," Dickson repeated the story of Archie's Mexican birth with some modifications: "…The white man [Grey Owl's father] who has married an Apache is killed in a feud, and in revenging him his eldest son is also killed. The little boy [Grey Owl]…is left alone with his Indian mother. Though he is part white, he never remembers this. He grows up an Indian…"

At first Archie was speaking to half-filled houses at the London theatre Dickson had booked for two weeks. But by the end of the first week he was playing to full houses and police were needed to control the crowds. Dickson booked the London theatre for another two weeks at the end of December, following previously scheduled lectures across England and Scotland. Grey Owl was equally popular outside of London, so he continued to tour until February 8. In four months he gave over 200 lectures to nearly a quarter million people, and autographed between 100 and 300 books after each performance. The excitement generated by Grey Owl in England was comparable to Beatlemania in the 1960s.

Although Pony was not present, she (as Anahareo) was an unforgettable image to those who attended the lectures. She was the heroine of *Pilgrims of the Wild* and the leading lady of the beaver films. Dickson became concerned when he got hints that all was not well with the couple. He also began to realize Archie had a drinking problem. "I could not have such a man giving way to the bottle, or letting it be known that the great romance which had inspired him had broken up," Dickson said.

One of the stops on Archie's lecture tour was his hometown of Hastings. The local newspapers reviewed his talk and described his performance in detail. The theatre darkened, the articles said, and then a lone spotlight fell on a tall, hawk-faced man clad in buckskins, wearing moccasins and a single eagle feather in his hair. As the man walked across the stage, an unseen gramophone played the opening bars of Beethoven's *Moonlight Sonata*. The man raised his hand in greeting and the music stopped. He said "How Kola" (actually a Sioux greeting rather than Ojibwa) to the 1,400 people in the audience.

At least three people in the Hastings audience recognized Grey Owl as Archie Belaney, but they all kept his secret. Two of them were his aunts, Ada and Carrie, who attended his afternoon talk and visited with him afterwards over tea at a hotel. When he returned home, he wrote to the hotel manager to ask for the address of the Misses Belaney, stating that they were good friends who had entertained him during the war days and again at the time of his lecture. His aunts did not tell anyone that Grey Owl was their nephew. As Ada wrote to a local paper following Archie's death, they admired his transformation, which allowed him to "carry on his work among the Red Indians more easily and naturally."

The third person who recognized him was the sister of his childhood friend, George McCormick. She commented to a friend that if Grey Owl was not Archie Belaney she would eat her hat, but she evidently said nothing to anyone else.

Public support for Grey Owl's conservation and environmental message was a precursor of the protest movements of the 1960s — although Archie didn't ask his listeners to take direct action such as refusing to wear furs or pressing for environmental legislation. "When he strayed into these issues in his talks he was always plainly uncomfortable, speaking by the book rather than from his mind," Dickson said.

Canadian journalist Matthew Halton, who conducted a long interview with Archie in London, described him as "one of the most civilized men I have ever interviewed." Halton said that "few white Canadians have raised Canada's prestige over here so high as Grey Owl has done."

Archie told Halton that his main objective was to "save as much as possible of the wilds for the nation and for posterity," so that future generations would be able to drive into wilderness preserves "where animals and men live as they lived in earlier time." He said he was not sentimental over animals and did not oppose killing them for food. "I don't rush up to women wearing furs and tell them how wicked and cruel they are. I merely asked for a dignified approach to the animal world."

A woman named Betty Somervell acted as Archie's chauffeur during the last half of his tour and accompanied him on the ship back to Canada. They first met when she volunteered to drive him to his next lecture after the car he was travelling in had a minor accident. As Archie hated train travel, Betty agreed to continue as his driver for the remainder of his tour. Dickson was concerned that Archie — who seemed completely disinterested in money — might lose or waste all his earnings. So he asked Betty not to give Archie the cheque for his half-share of the lecture receipts until they were at sea.

Betty kept a diary of her experiences. She found the ocean trip difficult at times. On his arrival in England, Archie's luggage had consisted of two small bags. On his return, he had a trunk and eight large suitcases filled with gifts and purchases — including a gramophone with records and a feathered Plains Indian war bonnet. Betty said that travelling with the war bonnet was worse than travelling with a newborn baby. Archie refused to pack it in the trunk because he feared it would be crushed.

For the first few days on board ship, Archie drank heavily. Finally Betty had enough and soundly scolded him. He stopped drinking and started dictating sections of his next book to her. Betty wrote in her diary, "He went at about 60 miles an hour and I had to scribble away in longhand trying to keep up. He used to sit straight up on the edge of a hard chair, and smoke little black cigars and dictate all night."

Archie was now making about $30,000 a year from book sales and lecture fees. His first instinct was to give his money away to anyone he thought might need it. When he returned to Canada he made a will, on the advice of Park Superintendent Major Wood, and arranged to have a trust company manage his money.

Archie spent a short while in Toronto and Ottawa before returning to Saskatchewan. Unfortunately for both his reputation and his attempts to get funding for two new films he wanted to make, he appeared drunk in public on several occasions. He didn't head home until he was told that his daughter Shirley Dawn was in hospital with pneumonia. On arrival in Prince Albert, he went on another binge and had a terrible row with Pony.

Archie's employers were not pleased with the reports of his drunken behaviour. They considered firing him, but reconsidered when they realized he had been on unpaid leave during his trip to England. Also, they recognized how much valuable publicity his tour had given to Canada's National Parks.

When Archie arrived back at Lake Ajawaan early in the summer of 1936, he completed work on *Tales of an Empty Cabin*, a book of short stories. The first part of the book dealt with the animals and people of the Mississagi River, and the last third was about Lake Ajawaan and the beavers.

Pony didn't join Archie at Lake Ajawaan until September. By then they realized they had grown far apart. They tried unsuccessfully to recapture the spirit of the earlier years of their marriage. Archie was so busy writing his book that he barely took time to play with Dawn and the beavers, let alone pay attention to Pony. She later said she might have been content to stay at Ajawaan had she been older, but at her age (she was more than 18 years younger than Archie) she found it impossible.

Later that fall, while visiting Archie and Pony at Lake Ajawaan, Betty Somervell and her husband witnessed the end of the marriage. On the final day of the Somervells' visit,

Pony and Dawn accompanied them as far as Prince Albert. Archie and Pony solemnly bid farewell, each promising to come to the other's aid if the need arose. The canoes put out from shore. Pony turned and gave a final wave with her paddle. She never saw Archie again.

Almost as soon as Pony had left, Archie decided to remarry. He had at least two women in mind as possible replacements for Pony, one in Regina and the other in Ottawa. In a letter to Lovat Dickson dated November 20, 1936, Hugh Eayrs wrote, "Grey Owl wants to settle down and get married! He tells me of a lady in Regina...in whom he is extremely interested...Unfortunately, she...is married at present."

Dickson replied, "The news you give me of his matrimonial intentions is — I don't know what to say — amusing, appalling, amazing...We shall not announce a fresh marriage, if there is one, in England, for Anahareo is just as much a hero to the English public as Grey Owl."

The second woman Archie was interested in was Yvonne Perrier. Archie had met her the previous spring while visiting with his friend Lloyd Roberts in Ottawa on his return from his British tour. He returned to Ottawa to court Yvonne, and in late November he asked her to marry him. She accepted, and they were married in Montreal in early December 1936, although he was still legally married to Angele. (Archie and Pony's marriage had remained common law.)

The record of Archie and Yvonne's marriage states that

he was Archie McNeil, son of the late George McNeil of Arizona and his wife, the late Catherine Cochise. Little is known about Yvonne except that she was of French-Canadian origin and was working in the home of a female doctor in Ottawa when they met. Archie was 48 and Yvonne was likely considerably younger.

Later that year Archie also renewed his passport under the name Archie McNeil, although his military pension cheques still came to Archie Belaney and he was listed as Archie Belaney in his Parks Canada personnel file. He used the name Grey Owl only as an author and lecturer.

Two months after their wedding, Archie and Yvonne went to Abitibi, Quebec, to make a film about winter wilderness travel for Archie's second British tour. Yvonne took enthusiastically to winter camping, dog sledding, and snowshoeing, but Archie's health was now so poor that he was exhausted at the end of every day of filming. His exhaustion shows in several scenes in the film.

After he returned from Abitibi, Archie was upset to find that Charlie the moose, his closest animal friend next to Jelly and Rawhide, was dead. Charlie evidently died of an illness. His body was "all skin and bone."

In June, Archie and Yvonne went to Biscotasing to make a film of a two-week canoe trip on the Mississagi River. Following completion, including the editing process in Toronto, Archie and Yvonne returned to Lake Ajawaan, where they made a new leather outfit for his upcoming British tour.

This outfit was much more heavily decorated than the one for his first tour — it looked like a beaded suit of armour. They also received one thousand visitors at Ajawaan to see the beavers that summer.

The second tour was an even greater success than the first, but Dickson did not enjoy it as much. He felt that some of the happy excitement had gone out of the venture. Grey Owl "behaved more like a successful dramatic impresario than a man with a mission," Dickson said. Despite Dickson's disappointment with Archie's new marriage, he gave "the new Mrs. Grey Owl" credit as "a charming, pretty, quiet, self-contained girl who appeared to manage Grey Owl very competently." Dickson had got Archie to agree to present Yvonne as his secretary, so they didn't have to tell the public of his break-up with Anahareo.

Dickson hired a young Canadian, Ken Conibear, to manage the tour. A typical Grey Owl performance, Conibear said, included the opening with the "Moonlight Sonata," but this time an organist provided the music instead of a gramophone. Then the curtain rose on selected newsreel scenes. Finally the curtain dropped again and a solemn voice announced Grey Owl.

"The face is noble," Conibear wrote. "In the hawk-like nose, the high cheekbones, the heavy lines, the parted and braided hair, the stern expression, there seems typified all you have ever heard of the noble character of the Indian of old...His voice is deep resonant, rhythmic. His diction is a strangely pleasing mixture of Canadian colloquialisms, classical idioms, and almost Biblical phraseology..."

Archie performed superbly. Although each performance was slightly different, each had the same elements. They included dry humour, self-belittlement, exaggeration, and glorification of native people and the Canadian North. And each performance concluded with a plea for understanding and compassion.

The highlight of Archie's second British tour was a royal command performance at Buckingham Palace. Protocol indicated he should be in place when the royal party entered, but he insisted that the lecture was off unless he could come in after they were seated. Dickson and other officials gave way to avoid making the dispute public.

Archie entered, flung up his right arm in salute, and greeted King George VI, saying, "I come in peace, brother." The King smiled and bowed his head slightly. During his talk Archie addressed himself almost exclusively to the two princesses, Elizabeth (now Queen Elizabeth II) and Margaret Rose. When Dickson gave Archie the previously-arranged signal to end his talk, Archie kept on talking because Princess Elizabeth jumped up and cried, "Oh, do go on."

At the end of the command performance, Archie touched the king's shoulder and said, "Goodbye brother. I'll be seeing you."

Archie gave 140 lectures between October and December of 1937. Dickson recalled his last meeting with

Archie, who was "haggard with fatigue." He rarely slept more than an hour or two during the night and only took brief cat naps during the day. He also appeared to have been "fighting off the strain with the bottle." Archie told Dickson that he would never return to England. He invited Dickson to visit him at Lake Ajawaan. Dickson accepted, but "somehow I knew it would never happen...on the last night before he sailed...we each spoke as one would speak to a dying companion from whom one was about to part forever."

Chapter 9
The Myth Explodes

espite Archie's obvious exhaustion and poor health, he did not immediately return home after his British tour of 1937. He went on a three-month lecture series in central Canada and parts of the United States, criss-crossing the Canadian–American border several times. Archie's agreeing to the North American tour at that time is puzzling, since he was almost at the breaking point. During the tour he commented, "Another month of this will kill me. If I am to remain loyal to my inner voices, I must return to my cabin in Saskatchewan." During the last weeks of his tour he ate little more than two raw eggs per day.

Archie gave the final lecture of his central Canadian

tour at Massey Hall in Toronto on March 26, and then returned to Saskatchewan, where he gave one last lecture in Regina. Yvonne was also ill by this time. She had surgery in a Regina hospital while Archie continued on to Lake Ajawaan.

A couple of days after he arrived home he phoned the park office in Waskesiu to report that he was ill. A ranger brought him out to the hospital in Prince Albert, where Archie was diagnosed with pneumonia.

Archie did not seem seriously ill when he entered hospital late Sunday night, but on Tuesday night he developed a fever. He quickly became delirious and was in a coma by midnight. A visitor that evening overheard him tell a nun in the Catholic hospital he was in, "The only religion I have is the great outdoors, the trees and wildlife of the forests." About 3 a.m. Wednesday, the hospital phoned Park Superintendent Major Wood to tell him there was little hope for Archie's recovery.

Pony didn't learn that Archie was in hospital until the night before his death. Her first impulse was to rush to his bedside, but she was told that he was sleeping so decided to wait until morning. The next day she bitterly regretted that decision when the doctor told her that Archie had been asking for her and that now he was in a coma. He died on April 13, 1938.

The day after Archie's death the North Bay *Nugget*, a northern Ontario newspaper, printed the story of his true identity — a story the editor had held for three years. Back in

The Myth Explodes

1935 a young *Nugget* reporter had gone to Temagami after receiving a tip from a local resident. The reporter met Angele Belaney, who told him she had seen a picture of Grey Owl in a newspaper and that he was her legal husband, an Englishman named Archie Belaney. The *Nugget* editor decided against publishing the story, both then and two years later when he received confirmation from another source that Angele's story was true. The editor said he kept the secret because the Grey Owl story was a positive one in a world with so many serious problems. He felt that exposing Grey Owl's true identity would destroy the good work he was doing. The *Nugget* story quoted both Angele and Bill Guppy. Bill said, "The next thing we knew he was Grey Owl. We have watched with interest and amusement his career as a writer and lecturer. But we will never forget him as the young Englishman whom we liked very much."

When the story came out many newspapers replaced the glowing obituaries with sensational headlines. "Grey Owl, the imposter of the century," one said, while another called him "the Modern Bluebeard." Another headline read "The Greatest imposter in literary history."

Pony was devastated. "I thought of all the worries, the near-starvation that we'd gone through after he quit the trapline, of his writing and lecturing, of all the time and effort he'd put forth towards conserving wildlife, and it was awful to think that it was all for nothing," she wrote. "Archie's public felt they'd been gypped and that he had only been after the fast buck. This wasn't true, for a great part of the money he had made was spent furthering his conservation ideas — his two films alone had cost $40,000."

She had never doubted Archie's story about his past and initially did not believe the *Nugget* story. "When, finally, I was convinced that Archie was English," she said, "I had the awful feeling for all those years I had been married to a ghost, that the man who now lay buried at Ajawaan was someone I had never known, and that Archie had never really existed."

Pony did not attend Archie's funeral. She thought it wouldn't be proper because Yvonne was still in hospital in Regina. The only family member in attendance was his five-year-old daughter, Dawn, who attended with Mrs. Winter, a woman who had regularly looked after Dawn during Pony's frequent prospecting trips. Archie was buried at Lake Ajawaan in a grave marked with a simple cross engraved, "A. Belaney" horizontally and "Grey Owl" vertically.

After several days, evidence supporting the *Nugget* story came from England. The editor of a Hastings area newspaper remembered the letter Grey Owl had sent to a local hotel asking for the address of two women who had entertained him while he was in Hastings during the war. He located Archie's aunts, but they initially refused to talk to him. Then, as they were shutting the door on him, the editor asked, "Can you just tell me what relation you were to Grey Owl?" One of them replied, without thinking, "He was our nephew."

After that Ada and Carrie Belaney reluctantly answered

a few questions. The editor corroborated their information by locating Archie's birth certificate and the certificate of his marriage to Ivy Holmes. Holmes stated that one toe on Archie's right foot had been amputated, and the funeral home in Prince Albert confirmed that Grey Owl did in fact have one toe missing.

Lovat Dickson, who felt that he and Grey Owl had been friends as well as business associates, was particularly shocked to hear the charges that Grey Owl was not who he claimed to be. "The saint was fast being turned into a mountebank," Dickson wrote. "I had so long been devoting myself to this man and his books that automatically I began to spend as much time in defending him as I had done in promoting him...I could not believe that he had deceived me...after all, there was nothing inherently impossible in being born in Hastings of an American Indian mother."

Not all of the newspapers vilified Grey Owl. The *Winnipeg Tribune* (April 20, 1938) wrote, "The chances are that Archie Belaney could not have done nearly such effective work for the conservation of wild life under his own name. It is an odd commentary, but true enough that many people will not listen to simple truths except when uttered by exotic personalities."

The *Times* (of London, England) published a long letter from Dickson, who said the public would soon tire of this "supremely unimportant topic" (Grey Owl's background). What would remain, Dickson said, were his achievements.

Dickson's letter stated, "He gave his extraordinary genius, his passionate sympathy, his bodily strength, his magnetic personal influence, even his very earnings to the service of animals…There lies the truth about Grey Owl, inseparable from the truth of Grey Owl."

Dickson eventually convinced Archie's aunts to talk to him by saying he would get the full story with or without their help and their talking to him could help ensure it was accurate. Now that he had to accept that Grey Owl actually was Archie Belaney, Dickson wanted to learn as much as possible about Archie's background. He wanted to explain Archie's transition to Grey Owl without making him look like a fraud. Dickson also met Archie's mother, Kitty Scott-Brown, who told him that Archie had spent several hours with her during his second British tour, "the happiest I have ever known." She confided, "He really did like me although he pretended not to."

In the summer of 1938, Dickson published *The Green Leaf: A Memorial to Grey Owl*. This book did much to restore Grey Owl's reputation as a great writer and conservationist. Major Wood, Superintendent of Prince Albert National Park, wrote in *The Green Leaf* that Grey Owl was a great man, whatever his background. Wood credited him with educating people about the disastrous effects of forest fires, trying to eliminate cruelty in trapping without being an opponent of the fur trade, and trying to help the native people regain some of their "old-time dignity and independence." Wood also commended Archie's stand against hunting unless it was for food. As Wood said, Archie particularly disliked "the destruction of a moose or elk by some fat millionaire" who hunted purely to have a trophy head to hang in his hunting lodge and left the remainder of the animal behind in the bush.

A young Canadian woman who assisted Archie on his first British lecture tour said that the honesty with which he spoke about the need for conservation was above suspicion. Therefore, it never occurred to her to doubt his statements about his background. When it was later shown that he was not part native, she was reluctant to describe him as an imposter. As she said, "...an imposter is a hypocrite or a quack with devious ulterior motives, a person who misleads knowingly or is without qualification to advise. Certainly where his life and work were concerned he had earned the right to be respected and cleared of either epithet."

Epilogue

Despite his desire to divorce himself from his family and be reborn as a North American native, Archie Belaney was unable to escape the influences of his family. Like his father, Archie became an alcoholic with a weakness for attractive women and an inability to take responsibility for his children. Like his grandfather Archibald Belaney — as well as two of his grandfather's brothers — Archie became a published author. His grandfather wrote poetry in addition to being a successful businessman, and his great-uncle Robert was a clergyman who wrote a large number of theological books.

Perhaps Archie was most like his great uncle James, a physician who wrote poetry and a highly successful book on falconry. James described the affectionate relationship he had with one of his hawks, who would wait by his bedroom door when he was out in the evening and rub her beak against his cheek upon his return. James said he was "a true-born bachelor," but later married a woman half his age.

Between 1930 and 1936 Archie wrote four books as well as 25 articles for the Canadian Forestry Association magazine, *Forest and Outdoors*. His books were later published in almost 20 different languages. As recently as 1981 Grey Owl was the second best-selling Canadian author in the former Soviet Union.

The Government of Ontario recognized Archie Belaney's contribution by erecting a plaque in his honour in a Temagami provincial park in 1959. It said, "Alarmed at the rapid despoliation of the wilderness, the wanton slaughter of wildlife, and the threat to Indian cultural survival, he became an ardent conservationist."

The Parks Branch seemed reluctant to remember Grey Owl. It was not until the 1970s that Grey Owl's cabins in Riding Mountain and Prince Albert national parks were restored. An American couple were so impressed with Grey Owl's conservationist philosophy that they donated $750,000 in 1988 towards the preservation of the canoe routes to Lake Ajawaan and to maintain Beaver Lodge itself. Even today, the only way to reach Lake Ajawaan is by a combination of walking and paddling.

Archie, along with Pony and Dawn, are buried near the cabin on Lake Ajawaan. A plaque by their graves reads, "Say a silent thank-you for the preservation of wilderness areas, for the lives of the creatures who live there and for the people with the foresight to realize this heritage, no matter how."

Bibliography

Addison, Ottelyn. *Early Days in Algonquin Park*. Toronto: McGraw-Hill Ryerson, 1974.

Anahareo. *Devil in Deerskins*. Toronto: New Press, 1972.

Dickson, Lovat, ed. *The Green Leaf: A Memorial to Grey Owl*. London: Lovat Dickson Ltd., 1938.

Dickson, Lovat. *Wilderness Man: The Strange Story of Grey Owl*. Toronto: Macmillan, 1973.

Grey Owl. *The Adventures of Sajo and Her Beaver People*. Toronto; Macmillan, 1935.

Grey Owl. *A Book of Grey Owl*. Toronto: Macmillan, 1938.

Grey Owl. *The Men of the Last Frontier*. Toronto: Macmillan, 1932.

Grey Owl. *Pilgrims of the Wild*. Toronto: Macmillan, 1935.

Grey Owl. *Tales of an Empty Cabin*. Toronto: Macmillan, 1936.

Bibliography

Pink, Hal. *Bill Guppy: King of the Woodsmen.* London: Hutchinson, 1940.

Ruffo, Armand Garnet. *Grey Owl: The Mystery of Archie Belaney.* Regina: Coteau Books, 1997.

Smith, Donald. *From the Land of the Shadow: The Making of Grey Owl.* Saskatoon: Western Producer Prairie Books, 1990.

Acknowledgments

The information for this book comes from four main sources — Grey Owl's *Pilgrims of the Wild*, Anahareo's *Devil in Deerskins*, Dickson's *Wilderness Man*, and Smith's *From the Land of the Shadow*. The account of Archie's childhood and most of the information about his life with Pony is from *Devil in Deerskins*. The information about Archie and the Guppy family in Chapter 1 comes from the article by Bill Guppy's granddaughter, Julia Luttrell.

Some of the quotations from Grey Owl's writings are taken from Dickson and Smith. The others come directly from *A Book of Grey Owl*, which contains excerpts from all four of his books.

Two articles available on the Web provided useful reference material: Bill Steer's "Ralph Bice — Wilderness Legend" found on-line at http://www.northernontario.org/NorthernStories/RalphBice.htm and Julia Luttrell's "Grey Owl — Anatomy of a Myth" accessed at: http://www.northernontario.org/NorthernStories/GreyOwlJL.htm

About the Author

Irene Gordon lives along the Assiniboine River in Headingley, Manitoba. She has had a passion for history and writing since childhood. After a career as a teacher-librarian, she became a freelance writer in 1998.

She shares Grey Owl's love of canoeing in the wilderness and also enjoys skiing, sailing, hiking, swimming, and travelling. Above all, she enjoys spending time with her two young grandsons, Jesse and Riley.

Photo Credits

OTHER AMAZING STORIES

These titles are available wherever you buy books. If you have trouble finding the book you want, call the Altitude order desk at 1-800-957-6888, e-mail your request to: orderdesk@altitudepublishing.com or visit our Web site at www.amazingstories.ca

New AMAZING STORIES titles are published every month. If you would like more information, e-mail your name and mailing address to: amazingstories@altitudepublishing.com.